Tall Pines Animal Tales

Over 100 True Stories *of* Encounters with Animals

Enjoy a "wild" read! 2023
Beth Paragamian

Vaughn L. Paragamian

Vaughn L. & Elizabeth Paragamian

Cover & Interior Design by
Gray Dog Press, Spokane, WA

ISBN: 978-1-5323-7904-8

Printed in the United States of America

Contents

SCARY SITUATIONS

CAN'T BE EXPLAINED

DUMB STUFF

A MATTER OF SURVIVAL

A HELPING HAND

Tall Pines Animal Tales

Prologue

Throughout our private and professional lives we had many experiences with animals both wild and domestic. These experiences ranged from humorous to sad, but in all cases we learned something new.

This book has several objectives; first we want to provide you with stories of pure entertainment; second help you develop an appreciation of wildlife education and third help those that don't understand that the natural scene isn't the stereotypic peace and harmony. Wildlife struggle every day to survive and as mankind spreads into the habitats of wildlife there is going to be conflict. Most of the time wildlife are the losers. At the same time we can learn to appreciate God's creatures and do our part to ensure they have a place to thrive too.

To add diversity to this book we added a few stories from friends and some stories involving domestic animals and in particular our pets. We know some stories will make you sad, but we hope most stories make you at least smile. One last note these experiences were gained by being outdoors not in the house watching TV.

HUMOROUS STORIES

The Night Visitor

Ken Moffitt, Beth's paternal granddad, had many great stories of his life on Dan's Mountain in the Appalachians of western Maryland. Our favorite story occurred during a steamy summer night in the 1960s. Granddad had a very rustic two room tar paper cabin in which he used the second room for storage. Everything he needed was in the main room. However from time to time venomous copperheads and timber rattle snakes would find their way into the main cabin through the back room.

Although Granddad had never been bit by a snake, as a precaution, when he hiked he always carried a .38 caliber revolver and his special snake stick. Snakes caught in the cabin would get whacked with the stick, but the .38 was always handy when he was outside.

While cooking breakfast one morning, Granddad thought he saw movement near his bunk. He grabbed his stick and found a three foot timber rattlesnake that had found its way in. He quickly killed the snake and tossed it outside far from the cabin. The day was really heating up and the humidity was rising too. That evening he decided to sleep with the window next to his bunk open. That night a cool breeze was coming through the unscreened window. The memory of the day's event with the poisonous snake was still on his mind, so he placed his .38 close and his stick within reach. He soon fell asleep.

Granddad woke up with a start when something flopped on his chest. As quick as a cat he swiped the unwelcome visitor from his chest, reached for his .38 and drew the chain to his room light. With the revolver hammer cocked, his eyes were now searching for the creature that could have easily taken his life moments before. With the light on, he now had the upper hand, the .38 was his trump card and his advantage over any venomous snake that would be slithering through his cabin. Then suddenly out of the corner of his eye, he noticed some movement. He had it in his sights, he would blow it to smithereens and teach that serpent a lesson and it would never ever invade Grandad's cabin again. Shoot quick he thought before it escapes—shoot.

Ah, darn it's just a big old toad.

The toad had apparently hopped up a pile of firewood that Grandad had stacked outside the unscreened window by the bunk. He had forgotten about the pile of wood, but later moved it and then bought a screen for the window. Now, Granddad would not have any night visitors through that window.

The Great Crappie Study

When I worked in the Midwest a colleague told me an interesting story. He was in charge of a crappie study on a lake. A secretary knocked on his door and said there was a gentleman waiting to see him. He invited the man in and was impressed immediately. The visitor was well-groomed and dressed in a starched khaki uniform. Sewn to a shirt pocket on the uniform was a patch with a logo and the letters NSF. My friend naturally thought NSF stood for National Science Foundation.

The conversation started with the young man introducing himself as Stan and that he was doing crappie research. He wanted to know more about crappie research on the lake. My friend explained in detail the objectives and goals and the field tasks involved. Stan was favorably impressed and asked if he could tag along as my friend collected and released crappies. Stan needed to simply take a small blood sample from each fish. My friend had him explain what he was doing and it sounded legitimate. Stan was given a sampling schedule and he was on time every morning. My friend and his technician started to notice that Stan never changed vials for individual fish. Instead the blood samples were collected until a single vial was filled and labeled and then a new vial used. My friend thought that it wasn't important to Stan's study to have the blood samples separate for each crappie.

The summer ended and Stan explained he was finished and appreciated the help with his investigation. He said he was so pleased with the results he wanted to host a barbeque for everyone with the state agency. A date was set and a crowd showed up for the catered festivities and fun was had by all. Stan said good bye to the crowd and thanked my friend once more and drove off never to be seen again.

Several months later, an older gentleman walked into the office and introduced himself to my friend as Stan's dad. He asked if anyone had seen Stan lately and my friend said he hadn't since the barbeque. The man further explained he and Stan's mom were worried because Stan had serious mental problems and would pretend to be a professional of some sort or another, most recently a scientist. Stan had been missing for a long time and they needed to get him back in the mental hospital for treatment. My friend inquired about the party that Stan had arranged. "Oh that," said Stan's father, "I paid an enormous bill for a barbeque I knew nothing about until I got the invoice."

A Nice Catch of Crappies

Anyone fishing a Midwestern state soon learns you never leave a stringer of fish unattended by a boat or a dock. There is a demon lurking in those waters just waiting to take advantage of the inattentive or naïve fisherman who has stringered and left his catch in the water. That demon is the snapping turtle. I have caught snappers up to 40 pounds in Wisconsin and saw one much larger.

A high school friend of mine told me this story back in the early 60s. He and his dad were having a great day of catching nice black crappies off a dock in a lake in northern Wisconsin. They were putting their catch on a metal snap and chain stringer that could hold more than one fish on a snap. They had their stringer attached to the dock about twenty feet closer to shore. He said they were well aware of snapping turtles that could snatch their catch any minute so from time to time he would check the string of crappies. He had no sooner checked the stringer and returned to fishing when he heard a commotion from the direction of the stringer.

Thinking it was just their catch flopping on the surface he didn't react at first until his dad asked him to go check. He casually walked to the stringer and saw a musky of at least 25 pounds with a mouth full of their crappies. He shouted to his dad who came running and then quickly he reached down to unhook the stringer from the dock expecting to pull their catch free. The musky swiftly got the upper hand by twisting like an alligator and unhooked the stringer just inches before he could reach it. He and his dad watched helplessly as the large musky swam off with their supper.

Freshwater Squid?

I promised myself many years ago that I would always be professional, but I would never take myself too seriously. So a light hearted laugh was always okay so long as the mood was right and safety never compromised.

While in a local grocery store one summer afternoon, I noticed a special on squid. I bought some and that weekend we ate squid, but two were left over. The next week, I started my night trawl fish studies on Lake Pend Oreille to monitor the abundance of young kokanee salmon. Usually I had my own staff plus one or two volunteers. It was then that I decided I would have some fun with the left over squid. It should be understood that there are no known freshwater squid in North America. They are saltwater creatures.

One evening we had one of our fisheries research managers assist in the intensive operation of sampling fish with a large 10 x 10 foot mid-water trawling net. The net is pulled through the water by a powerful 32 foot boat. The net is attached to steel cables and is lowered into the water and retrieved with powerful winches. When the net is brought to the stern of the boat, the catch is emptied into a large basin and the catch inspected. I quietly instructed a technician to drop one of the two squids into the net as it was being lifted into the boat. We emptied the haul of hundreds of young kokanee, thousands of opossum shrimp and one lone squid. "What is this?" our guest researcher said. "Why it's a squid, now how did that get in the water? It must have been discarded by a fisherman using it for bait."

I said, "Squid aren't used for bait, but maybe someone tried it."

I told the same technician to wait at least an hour and at least three miles from the last site and drop the final squid into the net. Several hours later another squid is in the haul. "Hmm," the researcher says, "A second squid. It is quite unlikely to catch the bait of a single fisherman. Vaughn, you may have collected a new species and a freshwater one at that. You have discovered something new, this calls for a publication."

"Yes," I said, "this is remarkable. I have never heard of a freshwater squid."

Before sunrise we completed our night time sampling and returned to the harbor. The boat and gear were all secured and everyone headed home to catch some sleep and get ready for the next night of sampling. Just before we all left, I asked the researcher if he would like the two squid. "No, you'll need them to taxonomically identify them and give them a scientific name."

I answered, "You can have them, I can always get more."

"What, get more?"

"Yes I can get more at the grocery store where I got these."

"You trickster," he said. "Now you know why I don't play poker."

What Squid Are Not Good For

Our friend Karen told us a story about a husband who wanted to inspire his wife into keeping a tidy refrigerator. Apparently, the man's wife had a habit of storing food in the refrigerator for days on end without either using it for meals or throwing it out. The unused food would eventually turn disgustingly moldy. He decided he would try to frighten her into maintaining a healthier refrigerator. The husband thought he had a great idea.

He took a raw squid and put it in a jar of old mayonnaise expecting that when she opened the jar the sight of the squid would scare her. Several days went by, before he asked his wife to please clean out the older spoiled food in the refrigerator. The next day she cleaned the refrigerator like it was new, but without a response. She went on with her daily work. The husband was puzzled, so he complemented her on the clean refrigerator, and then asked specifically about the aged jar of mayonnaise. Her response was, "Yes, I opened the jar and it didn't look any different than the contents of any of the other jars."

I wondered, there has to be a moral somewhere to this story.

The Mini-Van Dog

In 1991, we bought a border collie for our son. Each of our three children, as they turned twelve, was allowed to have a pet dog with the condition that they take care of it. Our son named the dog Panther due to the dog's color – jet black except for the white ruff of fur under his neck. The dogs traveled with us frequently as we had relatives on the East Coast and we lived in Idaho.

Panther did well traveling as long as he could lie on the floor on the middle section and hide his head under the driver's seat. He would not come out until we stopped for a rest stop break. On one long road trip from our home to Maryland, our family pulled into a rest stop. The children's job was to walk and water their dogs. Our son played fetch with Panther in the dog area when a brown mini-van parked next to our mini-van. It was identical to our vehicle in color and shape and model and it was closer to the dog area and blocked the view of our van.

The occupants of the van stepped out of their vehicle and stood by their open side panel door. I walked closer to the dog area and called to the three children and their dogs saying, "Time to get into the van." Panther started running toward the parking area to get to his spot inside our van. However all that he saw was the strangers van. As he galloped toward the open panel door, the group standing there scattered different ways as they saw this large black animal running straight at them. As we watched in surprise, Panther leaped into their van, flattened himself onto the floor and hid his head beneath the driver's seat. I hurried over to the shocked group and apologized profusely while explaining that our van looked exactly like theirs. Then I called to Panther to come out, but he was determined that he would not budge until the next rest stop. Vaughn came over and we called and pulled at his leash, but still he did not move. Finally, we pried the large dog from his burrow and carried him to our van where he promptly hid under the seat. Again we apologized to the other family and when we had everyone settled in our vehicle, we headed out in our van.

Three hours later we decided it was time to get supper. We left the freeway and looked for a restaurant. We found one that everyone liked.

Leaving the dogs in the van, our family filed into the dining area and headed for the nearest table – only to see that same family with the identical van sitting at the next table. They recognized us immediately and after laughing, the father said, "If we had known that we would meet you here, you could have left your dog in our van."

Mistaken Identity

Animals are frequently misidentified for others of similar characteristics. For example, while hiking a trail in Glacier National Park many years ago, we met two women from Germany. They warned us about a moose that was just a few yards downhill. The moose turned out to be a mule deer doe. Another time a man came into our office with a picture of an animal in a tree. He thought it was a pine marten. Whoops, it was an adventuresome marmot.

This story takes the cake. One morning one of the receptionists in the Panhandle Regional office of the Idaho Department of Fish and Game (IDFG) took a call from a woman who told the office employee about a remarkable crow. It showed up on their doorstep. She and her daughter had made a pet of it. The bird was unafraid of them and followed them around. It would even eat bird seed out of their hands. They made a comfortable cage for the crow and it would hang out in their back yard. However, the caller remarked this crow wasn't as bright as she heard crows were supposed to be, but it was still a lot of fun as a pet.

The receptionist explained it was illegal to have a protected species from the wild like a crow or raven for a pet. The woman said she was a recent transplant from California and wasn't aware of game laws. She and her daughter would bring it by the office to have someone release it so it wouldn't follow them home. However, they wanted to wash it one more time before it was released to the wild. A few hours later they arrived at the Panhandle Regional office with a freshly cleaned bird in a box. They peeked in and said goodbye and went out the door.

The box with the bird was given to the Duty Officer (DO) who brought the crow to the back where there were some trees for it to roost in. The DO turned the box on its side and slowly opened it. He gave the opened box a gentle heave to stimulate the bird to fly out. However, the bird flopped to the ground and a black.... chicken righted itself to search for grain and grit.

The Big One That Didn't Get Away

There was always something unique about the culture of Wisconsin residents. They love ice fishing. There may be three feet of ice on a lake and -20, but that won't stop a badger from walleye or northern pike fishing.

My cousin Ralph told me this story about walleye ice fishing – a whole day and part of a night. He was in college. Despite the frigid temperature, Ralph and his buddy headed out onto Lake Menomin, on the outskirts of Menomonie, Wisconsin. They had been fishing near the mouth of the Red Cedar River that contributes most of the water to Lake Menomin. Fishing with tip-ups was good and a few walleye were caught for the night's meal. A tip-up is a fishing rig that is placed over a hole in the ice and has a trip lever that flips a flag up when a fish takes the bait.

Wisconsin law prohibits fishing on some lakes after dark and it was approaching the time to pull the tip-ups off the ice when suddenly a flag went up – signaling a fish caught. The anglers were excited to finish the day off with one more walleye. They hustled to the tip-up, pulled it from the water and Ralph grabbed the line to set the hook and pull his fish in. He pulled hard, but his catch slowly pulled line out. It was big - maybe a musky. He fought the fish with his buddy standing by ready to assist. But, when he started to gain more line and get the fish close to the hole, the fish started to pull line out. It was just about dark now with just a bit of light and the tug of war continued.

It was past fishing hours, but surely a conservation officer would understand. No fisherman in his right mind would give up—not now—not after an almost two hour fight. Ralph was gaining line again so as he pulled and strained, he thought they would finally see the hooked behemoth. As Ralph got his quarry closer to the hole there was just enough light to see a large dark figure slide by the hole. The figure was too large to fit through their six inch hole. It must be a musky, no fish but a musky could be that large.

"Quick," Ralph said, "go back to the dorm and get a spud bar (a large steel chisel with a four foot handle) so we can make the hole bigger." Ralph's fishing companion ran to the car, drove to the dorm and returned 30 minutes later with a spud bar. The fishing team frantically chiseled the hole larger so the monster musky could be pulled through the hole. They had to be careful they did not cut the line with the sharp spud bar.

Ralph once again had the behemoth coming. It would be all or nothing now in near total darkness. The plan was for Ralph to pull as hard as he could and as the fish came up through the hole his buddy would wrap his arms around it. When his buddy had the fish secure Ralph would grab it too and both would heave it onto the ice.

"Here it comes," Ralph shouted. Yes indeed, the catch came through the enlarged hole perfectly. His fishing buddy grabbed it as it came up, Ralph let loose of the line and grabbed the lower section. The two heaved the catch onto the ice. Was it a record, was it a trophy?

The anglers were disappointed at the end result of the three hour struggle. It was a trophy… log, just a log. The river current had given the inanimate object life. If nothing else it makes a great fishing story.

The Foul Fowl

Many years ago (early 1950s), I visited a grade school friend's home to play. His normally cheerful mom was visibly upset. It seems they'd recently purchased a rather expensive talking bird and it learned some new words. My friend's dad, without his wife knowing, thought it would be funny to teach the bird some cuss words. Apparently he was a good teacher. Earlier in the day, my friend's mom had some ladies over for coffee and the hostess had a surprise for them - the family's new talking bird. She unveiled the bird and the ladies thought it was quite beautiful until my friend's mom started talking to it. It answered back with a string of profanity only a drunken sailor could match. When she became upset and told the bird to shut up it spouted off with a four letter f word followed by Y-O-U. She became tearful and hurried the bird and cage into another room and closed the door. Her friends thought they had enough entertainment for the day and left. I later learned the bird was given away, most likely to a bar patronized by seamen.

The Echo

Our son Jon is an electronic installer for a large satellite TV company and he travels through north Idaho for his work. He meets a lot of nice people and on one occasion was doing an installation while the family's grandmother watched. She looked on, was very quiet and did nothing to disrupt Jon's progress. After completing the electronic installation his next step, for record keeping, was to call in by phone, the equipment's security codes. It was very important that each code be the correct one for each device. After making phone contact with the company's recoding agent he began to read the code on the first device—A27GH7.

However, coming from grandma's direction, like an echo, he heard each letter or numeral repeated in sequence after he said it. Jon had to be precise and the continuous echo was disruptive. He looked to grandma and she sat with a stern look and stared back at Jon. So Jon continued, "7" and he heard the number repeated immediately "7", he looked at the elderly woman again, Jon turned away and said to his phone " J" and then he heard " J". He looked at grandma a third time and was about to question her about why she found it necessary to repeat after him when she said, "It's not me it's that bird in the cage back there."

Ants Anyone?

Many years ago we were on our way to Yellowstone National Park, from Iowa, and we had planned to visit friends in South Dakota. Our friends invited us to stay the night and we spent the evening in fun conversation. The next morning we were treated to pancakes, sausages and coffee for breakfast. The breakfast was great or so we thought. After we finished breakfast, we had our last cup of coffee. Suddenly, the lady of the household shrieked, "Oh yuck, look at all the ants in the syrup on your plate." The left over syrup on my plate was loaded with tiny dead ants.

My friend then held up the syrup container and said, "Look at all the ants. I wonder how they got in there?" We looked at the other plates and there were hundreds of dead ants on each. Until that time, no one had noticed the ants. Had they not said anything, we'd have gone on our way and never given it a second thought. Instead all we talked about on the way to Yellowstone was ants for breakfast and the benefits of the chiton diet. It may have promoted our fingernail growth. I also brushed my teeth that night much more rigorously than normal to make sure I removed all the ant legs from between my teeth.

Now, there are cooking recipes featuring ants, crickets, mealworms etc – times have changed.

More Ants

One summer Beth and I traveled to Barcelona, Spain, where I attended an international fisheries meeting that I helped organize. The meeting was held at a university located just outside Barcelona. Since we had to fund our own travel, it was important to cut expenses. So Beth and I stayed in a university dormitory room which turned out to have no air-conditioning. Accommodations were passable despite the hot weather. We slept with the unscreened bedroom window open and from time to time a stray cat would find its way into our dorm room. My single dorm bed was close to the window, while Beth's bunk was across the room.

One evening I woke up to what felt like sand in my bed. I didn't want to disturb Beth, so I didn't turn on a light. I could feel the tiny particles on the bed sheet that covered the mattress. So I vigorously brushed off what I thought was sand. I quickly crawled back in bed only to wake a few hours later to the feeling of sand on the mattress sheet again. This time I located my flashlight and there on the mattress sheet were hundreds and hundreds of dead ants. I brushed the dead ones off and they were quickly replaced with a new battalion of live ants. The dead ants were apparently killed as I rolled over them in my sleep. The ants were tiny and didn't bite. I looked on the floor and there were thousands of ants creeping around. I couldn't return to bed with the thought of sleeping with more ants. The next morning we marched into the university dormitory office and demanded a different dorm room.

An Unexpected Guest

The Wildlife Education Center in Coeur d'Alene was a great place for children and adults to learn about animals. There were live raptors, frogs, mammals and reptiles as well as mounted specimens. On occasion, young volunteers would not heed the warning to make sure the lids on the snake terrariums were on snug and weighted on the top. On rare occasions, one of the snakes would push hard enough to raise the lid a tiny amount and the snake would squeeze out of the narrow opening. The snakes were quickly found and put back in their respective terrariums. Snakes are far more powerful than most people think.

From time to time the Wildlife Education Center was used for civic group gatherings. While preparing the building to accommodate an upcoming event, Beth discovered the ball python was not in his terrarium. The five-foot long ball python was beautifully marked with a vermiculated color scheme. Beth and the five organizers who came to prepare for the event searched everywhere for the reptile, but could not find it. The few people who helped set up the event were sworn to secrecy—don't mention this dilemma to anyone. However, be on the look-out for "Bo".

All during the event, Beth and the helpers checked under tables, watched the room edges for anything moving and collectively held their breath. They expected anytime to hear someone scream or jump out of their seat after seeing the long snake. Finding the wayward reptile without an uproar was very important as there was one lady who almost refused to enter the building when she heard that snakes lived in the back storage room. However, the event went very smoothly, everyone had a great time and the guests departed – and still there was no sign of "Bo". Beth began to think that the snake was gone for good.

Just as Beth and the five volunteers were putting away tables and chairs and finishing the cleanup work, one of the workers yelled, "Guess what I found". The python had wrapped his long body around one of the legs of the full-sized mounted Woodland Caribou. After untangling the snake, the helpers still there held "Bo" and posed with it for photos. Then Bo went back into his cage with a more secure lock on its cage.

The Mouse Trapper

The Mississippi River is a phenomenal fisheries resource and is a beautiful body of water. The Iowa Department of Natural Resources has a research station on the Mississippi. A lot of good research has come out of that station, but pulling pranks was almost a daily event for two technicians stationed there in the 1980s. They were a hard working duo who also liked to take advantage of the unsuspecting and inexperienced. The next victim had just arrived, Tom a new technician fresh out of undergraduate school. Tom was a nice young man, but he didn't have a clue what he was in for.

The field station senior technician gave Tom an important assignment – to build a vermin proof screened storage area for the fishing nets. The area's dimensions were provided as well as the size of screening for the walls. The screens allowed air to pass through in case nets were damp and needed to dry. But the screen had to be fine enough to keep mice out. Mice can cause real problems, because for whatever reason they chew on net web and the holes are time consuming to repair. Tom built the net room and was very pleased with his work. Dimensions were perfect, the screen was tight and it was a sight to see.

Tom proudly showed his product to the two senior technicians and they approved. However, they asked, "Is it mouse proof?"

"I think so," he said.

"Only one way to find out," the senior men said. "Place a single mouse trap in the room and check it in the morning".

So a single mouse trap was baited with cheese, placed in the room and checked the next morning. There in the trap was a dead mouse. Tom was told to check for holes or an entry way that would allow a mouse to get in. Tom checked and looked and checked again, but he could not find a way a mouse or even a fly could get into his new net room.

It was then suggested maybe the mouse was in the room while he was constructing it. "Okay," he said, "I will rebait the trap and we'll see."

The next morning his trap did not catch one mouse, but two mice. How unusual the crew thought to catch two mice in one trap. It is possible, but very unusual. Tom searched again for a hole and found none. How were these mice getting in? This room was perfect. However, the senior technicians explained as perfect as this room appears, it is useless unless you can keep mice out. So once again Tom rebaited the trap to rid the room of the vermin once and for all. As soon as all of the mice were removed, then his project would serve its purpose.

The third morning was another surprise. Tom checked his trap and in it were not one, not two, but three mice. This must be a record. Three mice in one trap – that has to be in Ripley's "Believe It or Not". No one had ever done that. Tom reset the trap and the next morning there were no mice in the trap. His project was voted mouse proof and he had set a record at the same time – three mice in one trap.

Fall came and the annual statewide fisheries meeting was held. Informational presentations were provided by biologists, educational work-shops and an annual softball game played – region against region. The final night was attended by all state fisheries employees as there was an awards event. Tom was called to the front and center where he was awarded a plaque – a plaque with a mouse trap and three rubber mice. Then the prank was revealed. Tom's net room was mouse proof from the start. The mice were caught and placed in his traps before he checked them in the morning by none other than Tom's two superiors. A year later, Tom took his talent back to Illinois and probably pulled pranks on unsuspecting novice employees.

The Soap is Free

There is no end to the number of skunk stories. My friend Ned told me a good skunk story about when he and a friend were teenagers in Colorado. They decided to spend the weekend at the friend's family cabin in the beautiful high country. They brought along the family dachshund and were happy to finally arrive after a long journey. As they got out of the car, the dog burst for the cabin and crawled under it. A moment later a terrified dog emerged yipping and stinking of skunk. With no tomato juice or soap to clean the dog, the two boys doused him with gallons of water, but to no avail. They decided that they had to drive to the nearest grocery store for some high-powered soap and tomato juice to clean the pet.

While searching for the soap and tomato juice, the two boys started to draw attention to themselves. Customers avoided them, made faces and held their noses. The boys were puzzled, they believed only the dog smelled, not them. A clerk soon approached and asked them to leave.

"Not until we get some soap and tomato juice," one of the boys explained.

Soon the manager walked up to the boys and further instructed them to leave. He would find the products they needed. Just leave. The boys walked out and waited on the sidewalk. The manager quickly met them and gave them the soap and tomato juice – for free. As the manager slipped back into the store he added, "By the way I added some deodorant for you guys - use it and please don't return."

Skunk House

Skunks not only cause problems by getting into garbage and bowls of pet food, but they also have a distinct odor. Working for fish and game agencies my entire career had many benefits, however there were also some drawbacks due to the public's expectation. One expectation in Iowa as well as in Idaho was nuisance animal removal or in some cases execution.

In the mid-1980s on Thanksgiving evening, I got a call from a country neighbor for help to remove a skunk from his basement. To this day, I don't know how the skunk got in the basement, but when I stepped into their home, it smelled like the skunk had been in every room of the older home. The home was so old, it had a foundation made of limestone blocks.

After I arrived with a 12 gauge shotgun in hand my neighbor brought me to the basement. We tried to think of every way we could to persuade the skunk to go out a window we opened, but to no avail. I'd have to shoot it. Unfortunately for the skunk, life in the neighbor's house was short lived. The dead skunk was scooped up with a shovel and dumped into a burlap bag. It was also my job to dispose of the skunk which I did in the woods nearby. The neighbors were extremely thankful to rid the house of the skunk. I had coffee and cookies with the neighbors afterward. I remember the coffee wasn't bad, but the cookies had a suspicious aftertaste.

I drove the short distance to my home and was immediately ordered out of the house. My coveralls had taken on the skunk's odor and I stripped down in the evening darkness and hung my coveralls in the woods. I soon became the local skunk removal guy due to this successful skunk ordeal.

Can Baby Skunks Spray?

One of my biologists with IDFG was the lucky one for the day for the fish and game "gopher" assignment, the DO. His day was going smoothly with a few calls about fishing, until a woman brought in a nearly dead baby skunk. She found the small animal in her yard and the only explanation was it may have been hit by a car or a dog roughed it up. Since she really didn't want it in her possession she thought perhaps she'd take it to Fish and Game and they'd either rehabilitate it or put it out of its misery. Ryan, the fisheries biologist, looked at it and could see that the baby skunk was just barely breathing. Feeling sympathy for the ailing little creature, he wanted to humanely euthanize it. Handling it should not be a problem since the skunk was young. The lady convinced Ryan young skunks couldn't spray because that special gland was not yet fully developed.

Shooting it was out of the question since the office was in town, near a school and shooting it would get blood all over. Ryan decided to drown the nearly comatose animal. He found a six gallon pail, filled it with water and placed the skunk in it. He then took a big stick and pushed the skunk under. Once the skunk's nose was immersed, the animal instantly revived. The skunk burst up from the water, climbed the stick and sprayed Ryan. The battle was on. The skunk was fully awake now with a will to survive and Ryan with a will to finish the job. Man prevailed, but not before being sprayed several more times. When Ryan returned to the office, he was immediately asked to leave due to the skunk odor he was carrying. Ryan went home to clean up, but the only vehicle that was available was the office work truck – a brand new work truck. Since this was a work related incident and Ryan did not want to use his family car, he took the new truck home. When he reached his home he discovered there was no hot water, but he cleaned up and came back to the office with the work truck.

The following morning I was scheduled to meet the Fisheries Bureau Chief at the Spokane airport with our new truck and show him around our study area. However, my enthusiastic anticipation of picking up the Chief was shattered after one whiff of the interior of the new vehicle. I was able to borrow an old truck that had been used by the wildlife staff for a black bear study. The borrowed truck had the distinct odor of bear scent. However, the bear scent paled in comparison to the stench of the skunk. When the Chief quizzed me about the whereabouts of our new truck I said, "Did you know even baby skunks have a potent spray!"

I Don't Do Skunks

After we moved to north Idaho, I soon forgot about my skunk removal reputation in Iowa. I never anticipated dealing with skunks again, or so I thought.

On a sunny weekend afternoon, a rural neighbor called and asked if I would help her with a skunk. Like the nice guy that I am, I said okay. I walked to her home and there was an adult skunk stuffed into a small live trap used for squirrels. The trapped skunk was in tighter than sardines in a can. I decided I'd try my technique of releasing the trapped skunk using a tarp to shield myself from skunk spray. I held the tarp in front of myself and approached the skunk. I used a gloved hand to try to release the latch and gate on the trap. It didn't work. The release couldn't be moved because the skunk was stuffed into the trap so tight. Then I thought that since it can't move, it can't raise its tail to spray me. WRONG! I bravely reached down to try to release the latch again and got sprayed. There was no way I could get that trapped animal out of that tight a spot without opening it by hand and pulling it out physically. For concern of getting bit and perhaps contracting rabies, I decided to shoot it.

I helped the neighbor once more with a skunk and the result was the same – I got sprayed. On the third call of a trapped skunk I politely told the caller that it's your skunk. Sorry, but I don't do skunks anymore.

Will the Real Flower Step Forward

Our friend Gail told us that when she was a young girl, as a joke, her brother gave her a young skunk for her birthday. Gail named it Flower. The scent gland had been removed, but removing the scent gland didn't totally render the smell undetectable, but tolerable. The skunk was friendly, playful and became a popular pet with family and friends. When Gail married, she even had a few of her wedding pictures taken with Flower. Gail and her family were careful to make sure Flower never ventured outside without someone watching her.

One afternoon relatives, who were familiar with the pet skunk, were visiting and an uncle saw Flower outside and alone. Concerned that the little pet might wander off or get mauled by a larger animal, the uncle told Gail's dad that Flower was running free in the back yard. The patriarch immediately went outside to grab Flower and bring it back into the house. The skunk stood motionless as Gail's dad approached. He picked the skunk up and lifted it to his face. Just as he was about to say, "Bad girl sneaking out of the house," the pet impostor sprayed him in the face. The wild skunk was dropped to the ground and immediately waddled off to safety. A command decision was made that Flower was to have its own visible collar to identify her from lookalike phonies.

What Garage Doors Are For

Almost weekly our Fish and Game office would get a call from a new resident regarding a wildlife problem. One afternoon I was assigned to take wildlife, hunting or fishing calls from the public. I took a call from a lady that lived close to Post Falls, Idaho. She explained that a bobcat came into her garage nearly every night and ate her dog's food. She'd refill the dog bowl and the bobcat would come back again and empty the bowl of food. Even after she'd scare the bobcat away, it always returned. She wanted me to come trap the bobcat and move it to a distant location. I explained there may be an easier solution besides trapping it.

I asked, "Does the garage have a door?" She answered that of course, the garage had a door.

I then asked, "Does the door work?"

She replied, "Yes, the door works just fine."

I explained, "Then shut it. Every evening close the garage door and the bobcat will have to find food elsewhere."

"Oh, I hadn't thought about that," she said.

I Think I'm Going Blind

Our son Jon is an avid archery elk hunter and each season hikes miles and miles of the mountains of north Idaho to get his bull. In the 2000s, we frequently hunted a number of drainages in north Idaho. We set up camp 5 miles into our favorite drainage and hunted from there. One morning Jon hunted high up into one of the drainages and slowly worked his way back. Tired from the long trek up and now back down, he decided to take a snooze near a stream. He fell asleep in a prone position and when he woke up, he noticed a turkey vulture circling high above. Since Jon is a curious person, he stayed motionless as the raptor slowly circled lower and lower.

Eventually the bird landed on a branch directly above Jon. The bird stared, moving its head ever so slightly to get a better view, trying to determine if there was any life to the motionless body below. Slowly Jon moved his hand and pointed at the bird with his finger as if he was sighting in on a target. Jon immediately heard a flatuating (loud fart) sound come from the big bird. The turkey vulture was so freaked out it had defecated just as it gave flight. The white mass of bird poop plummeted toward the ground. Only the poop didn't hit the ground. The white substance splashed directly into Jon's right eye. Jon hustled to the stream and washed the foreign substance from his eye over and over. He kept washing the eye out.

Later that afternoon when we met he said, "Dad, I'm going to go blind," and explained what had happened. I told him he'd be okay, but to this day he has a disdain for turkey vultures. Oh, his vision's fine and for that Christmas Beth got him a Christmas ornament in the likeness of a turkey vulture. He did not like the Christmas gift.

The Dead Cardinal

For 39 years, I had permits from the U.S. Fish and Wildlife Service which allowed me to rehabilitate and release wildlife, to take care of permanently disabled wildlife for education and to collect dead wildlife species. The dead animals I collected were sent to taxidermists for museum displays for the Wildlife Centers that I managed. Many of the dead animals I collected were road kills that were not seriously damaged.

One summer morning in Iowa, Vaughn was driving in to work. He spotted a dead cardinal on the side of the road. The soft shoulder was narrow and the width was very misleading because tall grass on the edge concealed a sloping bank. When Vaughn saw the cardinal he thought of stopping to pick it up and give it to me because he knew that I was always on the look-out for new specimens for work. He thought better of it and continued on to work.

Just before noon, I loaded our three youngsters in the back seat of my car. I was headed to the County Wildlife Center and drove the same road where the cardinal was laying. I slowed down and pulled to the side of the road, however the right front and rear wheels dropped off of the hard surface. Just great, I thought, as I opened the driver's door and exited the vehicle. I opened the back door and instructed the three children to slide to the left side of the back seat and climb out. They did and the children and I surveyed the situation from the side of the road. I need to call a tow truck I thought.

Just then, a neighbor who worked in construction drove by and then stopped. As he climbed from his pickup truck, he casually remarked, "It looks like you need a little help". He pulled a tow chain out of his vehicle and walked toward my car.

"Thank goodness you came by," I responded, "I don't want Vaughn to come by and see us here." As luck would have it, Vaughn's vehicle came down the road. He stopped along the road and the first thing he said was, "I knew I should have picked up that dead bird." With the children and I watching, Vaughn took the chain from our neighbor and hooked it under the front of my car. He rolled down the driver window and as our neighbor drove his pickup forward, Vaughn steered my car back onto the roadway. I thanked our neighbor who then continued to town. I put our children back into the car and got ready to go to the Wildlife Center while Vaughn was planning to head home for lunch. "Oh wait," I said, "I need to go pick up my bird." I ran behind the car and grabbed the cardinal.

On closer inspection, the cardinal was not suitable for a museum mount so I fed it to a barred owl. The next day the owl regurgitated a beautiful pellet with the cardinal's red feathers and yellow bill visible. I have used this pellet for the past 35 years for wildlife education programs and it provided a very graphic example of prey items for raptors.

Fear the Snapper

To many Iowa families the most important event of the year is the Iowa State Fair in Des Moines. Many farm families have a difficult time getting away from the responsibility of operating their farms. Trusting or leaving the care of their farm to someone usually would only come once a year - for the State Fair. That's when many Iowans showed their livestock or produce at the fair. The State Fair occurred in August, one of the hottest and humid months of the year.

The Iowa Department of Natural Resources Fish and Wildlife Section had a wonderful exhibit each year. Native fish were displayed in large aquariums and the wildlife in pens. A question and answer booth was always staffed by fish and game professionals and staff even volunteered to work the fair booth during the fair. One of the wildlife exhibits included an in ground pool of 6 foot across and 3 foot deep. The pool housed a large beaver and a snapping turtle. Both animals were fed daily and they had shared that same pen at the State Fair for years without incident. The snapper often could be seen resting at the bottom of the pool, while the beaver sunned itself and on occasion would take a dip in the pool.

One warm afternoon, I was manning the booth with a fellow fisheries biologist when a woman approached us in a panic. She called our attention to the beaver and that it had dozens of flies on it. She wanted to know why we didn't do something to rid the beaver of the flies and cool it off. I explained that it wasn't practical to have someone swooshing flies away all day and that insect repellent could harm the animal. Besides, the beaver had a shaded place to go or it could take a dip in the pool. At that explanation, the fair visitor became even more upset and shouted, "How can the beaver go into that pool with a big snapping turtle in it. That beaver is in absolute fear of being bit by that nasty snapping turtle."

Some arguments you can never win, so I said nothing.

33

Grad School Fox Snake

My friends in graduate school knew I was interested in amphibians and reptiles and especially snakes. One evening I got a call from Dave, a fellow student. He said he had caught what he believed was a fox snake and would I identify it before he released it. I hadn't seen a fox snake in years and was looking forward to seeing it. The next morning I met Dave at the university grad student office, located in an old building, and he had a disappointed look. He held an empty shoe box and said the three foot long snake had escaped in the office. We searched the office and we could not find the serpent. Late that afternoon, as we were leaving the office, we greeted the night janitor, Earl. Earl had a noticeable gimp to his walk, because of an old farm accident. The injury never healed properly and kept him out of WWII. We never thought to tell Earl about the harmless missing fox snake.

Two nights later Earl had an encounter with the fox snake. He never knew what to expect to see in our office. There on the old fashioned water heater was a coiled snake. Earl thought the snake was made of rubber and placed there as a joke. As he reached for the snake, it began to shake the tip of its tail sounding like a rattle snake. Earl jerked his hand from the snake thinking he would get bit and die on the spot. He dropped his broom, ran from the office and called security about a loose rattlesnake. Security people entered the office and looked around, but no snake was found. They asked Earl if he was sure he saw a snake. "Absolutely, I saw a rattlesnake," he said.

The next day Dave and I were called into our major professor's office and asked to explain why a rattlesnake might be in the graduate office. We told him it was just a fox snake and it had escaped. The professor informed us that the janitor would not enter our office again until the snake was caught. And we had to promise that no live animals would be brought into the office again. That night Dave and I stayed in the office hoping to catch the snake. Late in the evening the innocent snake emerged from a large mouse hole in the wall. We caught him and he was released back where he was caught.

The next day we apologized to Earl and promised we'd have no more live animals in the office. He accepted our apology and explained that when he ran from the snake it was the first and only time in 40 years his leg worked right.

The Chicken Coop

In Iowa, we lived in a rural subdivision in the country. It was a new neighborhood with young families and many unsold wooded lots of 1 to 2 acres each. The lower road of the loop lane led to cabins by the lake where owners might come only on the weekends. Our three children, Laura, Jon and Karin, loved to explore the area with their friends of the same ages. The children built tree forts, made trails through the woods and played outdoor games that all children love. They discovered that one cabin on the lower lane had a small fenced area that held a few goats. They found out that the goats were not very friendly. They also discovered another building that held farmyard animals.

One day our three youngsters, along with two neighbor children, came back from their adventuring and were playing in our back yard. I noticed that the usually active kids were very quiet and moving slowly while they carried something in their hands. Quiet children? Of course I needed to check out what they were up to. I went outside and saw that each of the five kids had an egg cradled in their hands – a chicken egg. I asked where they found the eggs and the story emerged that during their explorations, they had found an abandoned chicken coop. There were a few chickens around the area, but they could not find anyone who took care of the fowl. They had even knocked on the doors of the nearby cabins, but no one answered. The kids went into the coop and saw these eggs and were worried about them. The kids thought they should take care of them and help them hatch.

I explained to the concerned youngsters that the coop, chickens and eggs did belong to someone, probably one of the weekend lake front cabin owners and that they needed to take the eggs back right away and put them in the coop exactly where they found them. The children nodded their agreement and slowly and carefully trudged down the lane toward the coop. When Vaughn came home from work, I told him about the great "egg caper" and that the children returned the eggs. The unknown owner probably wouldn't even know that the eggs had been borrowed.

A few days later Vaughn answered the phone and it was a call from the irate chicken owner. He told us that he would appreciate it if our children stayed away from his coop. Vaughn apologized for the kids and then questioned the man further. How did he know it was our children and not others in the neighborhood? "They wrote their names on the underside of the eggs," replied the man. It turned out when the 5 children were planning to hatch chicks, they each labeled their egg with their first name. "I don't know who the other two children are," said the man, "but I know your family." Oops, we did not know if that was a good thing or a bad thing. The next day, Vaughn took our three children down to the man's cabin and had them apologize in person.

A Chipmunk Tail

My step father loved his cat Pete. So whenever we traveled to northern Wisconsin on vacation, the cat came with us. However, the cat was never let loose outside. In fact it was always tethered on a rope or leash.

Chipmunks were plentiful and I'm sure they could not wait to see Pete the cat. Pete was tethered to the same tree each year where he had space to move and not get tangled. If it rained, Pete could reach shelter on the porch. The chipmunks teased Pete by getting close and taunting him by bouncing back and forth or slowly walk toward him. Pete would slowly ready himself for an attack on a dead run and the chipmunk would scurry just out of range. Pete would hit the end of his tether and his head would snap back while the rest of his body continued forward. The chipmunks would dance back and forth enjoying every bit of the action. When Pete would return to the porch, the chipmunks would repeat their skit until Pete tired of it. The result was always the same.

One morning my step father decided he would do things differently. He changed the location of the tether so Pete's range was extended to the chipmunks' hole. Soon a chipmunk emerged from the hole and started to taunt Pete. It approached Pete in the usual manner dancing back and forth. When Pete took off to give chase this time was different. Pete caught the chipmunk and the chipmunk was surprised. But, eventually the chipmunk escaped and ran like there was no tomorrow for his hole with Pete close behind. Just as the chipmunk reached his hole, Pete made a final lunge with his right paw going into the hole. There Pete sat for the rest of the morning looking very determined. Pete would not let go of whatever he had. It wasn't until mid-afternoon that Pete pulled his paw from the hole. In his paw was his prize – a chipmunk's tail. Pete played with the tail for the rest of the day and then the next. It was two days later that we saw a tail-less chipmunk. With its' body part now Pete's trophy the chipmunk would not go further than a few feet from its' hole.

The moral of the story is don't push your luck because you may lose your tail.

Grilled Squirrel

A pastor once told me, "Never one up another's story." For a story teller that is hard to do, but I was one upped myself by a female acquaintance. I told her a story about a rabbit that I almost accidentally scorched. I've burned wood during winter for almost 40 years. When we lived in Iowa, I used the logs from fallen trees on farm ground, piled the brush and burned it at the appropriate time. One afternoon it was safe to burn a brush pile, so I doused the 5 foot tall by 15 foot long brush pile with gas and lit it. The gas ignited the dry branches and I had an instant fire. Out of the blaze came a rabbit running as fast as a bullet. I believe that rabbit is still running.

The other story teller laughed at my tale and proceeded to tell me a better one. Seems it was time for her and friends to have a spring barbeque. Their gas grill hadn't been used since the previous summer. Everything was set; the hot dogs and hamburgers were ready and the condiments in place. My friend said with a single motion she entered a lighter into the grill as the gas valve was opened. There was an explosion as the gas ignited, the lid flew up and a terrified squirrel burst out of the grill. Its nest instantly caught fire and a hole it had chewed in the gas line detonated another fire. Someone acted quickly and shut the gas valve off as the grill went up in flames from the rubber hose and all the debris the squirrel had stashed in it. The beautiful red paint on the grill was scorched and hoses melted, the grill was a total loss. The following year the new grill was checked before the spring barbeque.

The Acrobatic Fox Squirrel

My friend Larry told me a story of an acrobatic squirrel he watched while hunting whitetail deer in his native Michigan. Larry waited silently under a huge red oak one autumn morning waiting for a nice buck to wander past. He heard a squirrel crawling up and down the rough barked tree that Larry was sitting under. Then the squirrel came into full view still hanging on to the side of the tree. It was a burly fox squirrel with a large acorn in its mouth. The squirrel was startled at the sight of Larry and dropped the acorn from its mouth. The squirrel didn't want to leave the nut there on the ground nor did it want to leave its safe perch. So after releasing its front feet from its firm grip on the tree bark, it slowly stretched its body toward the acorn. It stretched, and stretched and stretched and just as it had grabbed the acorn and got it back in his mouth the squirrel's hind legs lost their grip on the tree. The squirrel did several perfect forward rolls scoring a 10 on each successive role until it tired of the forward rolls, righted itself and scampered away. For the rest of the day Larry could have cared less if he saw a buck because he spent most of the day laughing at what he had seen. Hmm, I wonder if that squirrel escaped from a traveling circus.

The Peeping Snake

There was always something going on at the county park where Beth worked and Saturday afternoon was no exception. I was selling fire wood and as I passed from one camp site to another I noticed a bit of commotion at one end of the camp ground. There were two privys; a men's and women's. I noticed a lineup of men and women at the men's privy. For some reason the women didn't want to use the women's pit toilet.

I asked the crowd, waiting to use the men's privy, what was wrong with the women's privy. The women were not afraid to speak out. One lady said, "There's been a snake in the pit toilet all morning and afternoon and it won't come out."

"Yes, and when you open the door it pokes it's head up and peers over the toilet seat and then goes back down," another explained.

"We can't go in there. What if he decides to leave when one of us is sitting on the toilet, it would have to crawl between our legs. Can you imagine what it would be like to be doing your job on the toilet and have a huge snake crawl between your legs?"

"Besides, it may be a rattlesnake and bite a butt," another woman said.

"No," I said, "that would be a bit too exciting for me too." All along some of the younger boys were having a time of it laughing at the women. When I quizzed the boys, none knew anything about the snake. I walked over to the privy and knocked on the closed door. There was no response from inside.

"No kidding Vaughn, no one will use it. Can you do something?" asked one woman.

"Yes, I'll see what I can do." So I cautiously looked over the open toilet seat and after shining a light into the pit I saw a four foot long bull snake. I took a long rope from my truck and cut a 10 foot sapling from the nearby woods. I then fashioned a noose at the end of the pole. The crowd followed me from the privy to the woods and back to the privy. The toilet pit itself was at least eight feet deep making it awkward for me to maneuver the long pole and noose down into the toilet seat. Once in, I slipped the noose around the snake's head and gently pulled the noose tight. Now I just had to back out of the privy and withdraw the stick, noose and traumatized bull snake. The crowd around the door of the pit toilet started screaming and some were cheering as I backed out of the structure with the snake dangling from the noose. The snake shook its body wildly trying to escape. As I walked toward the end of the campground holding the pole and the captured snake, the crowd parted in front of me.

"Are you going to kill it?" someone asked.

"No, he's more afraid of you than you are of him," I said.

"I'll release the snake in the wetlands so the boys won't have a chance to torment it after I leave." As I walked to the water's edge, once again a line of people followed me. I released the snake and it took off like it was late for dinner, not hesitating to look back. I heard over and over how clever I was and I was the hero for the day, especially when bathroom facilities were involved.

Case of the Smelly Woodchuck

My fascination with fish and wildlife started at a very young age. To extend that interest I tried my hand at taxidermy. One afternoon I got a call from a friend who said he had shot a large animal that was digging a hole under his family's home. He asked if I would come over and identify it. It was a woodchuck. His mother offered to pay all expenses if I would stuff it. It was a deal. I took the animal home and skinned it and ordered eyes and a body from a taxidermy company. A few weeks later I had the straw body and glass eyes and finished the job.

Being a novice, I didn't prepare the pelt quite right, but the finished animal looked very real posed sitting up on its hind legs with its front feet holding a walnut. However within a few days, my taxidermy project started to smell of rotten meat and my mother demanded that I get rid of it. I brought the upright mount to my friends and explained my disappointment in not doing a good job in preserving the hide. Before long three more buddies showed up and admired my taxidermy work regardless of the smell.

My friend's house was located on a major county road. His home was concealed from the highway by a thick row of tall bushes along the property boundary. That section of highway was a no passing zone. One of us had the bright idea of setting the woodchuck in the middle of the highway and watching the reaction of the drivers and passengers in cars passing by. Most drivers passed by the woodchuck carefully as to not disturb it, while a group of older ladies were so fascinated that they backed up traffic a quarter mile behind them. Drivers beeped horns to get the traffic moving and tempers were rising because of the traffic jam. Finally the women moved on with smiles from their wildlife encounter.

The most comical sight was when a man pulled his car over to the soft shoulder on the opposite side of the road from us. He got out of the car and snuck through a thick hedge of bushes. When he was about 100 feet behind the motionless woodchuck, the man tiptoed down the center of the highway. His kids were watching intently from the rear window of the car and his wife peeked out an open side window. Slowly he approached the woodchuck and when he was 30 feet from it, the man ran at it screaming like crazy. Still the rodent didn't move. The man then bent down and looked it in the eyes. He burst into laughter and shouted, "It's stuffed and does it stink." He walked back to his car with the entire family laughing. The next driver didn't have a sense of humor. When he discovered it was a taxidermy mount he shouted, "If you kids don't get this off the road, I'm calling the cops." He drove off and when he was out of sight I scurried out and grabbed the smelly woodchuck.

The story of the smelly woodchuck didn't end with the road side warning. That same night we placed it on the seat of a caterpillar tractor at a road construction site. The tractor was in front of the home of two brothers who had joined us. The next morning they hid in thick cover and waited for the construction crew to come to work. The tractor driver casually walked to his machine and then was absolutely terrified at the sight of the woodchuck on the operator's seat. A fellow worker heard the commotion and saw the large creature on the seat. He grabbed a shovel and on the run swung and smashed the woodchuck off. He proceeded to beat it to smithereens as if it was a threatening predator. Not until the straw stuffing blanketed the road side did he realize it was a taxidermy mount. The demolished smelly woodchuck was kicked to the side. The construction workers last comment was, "Does that thing ever stink."

Many years later I made the mistake of telling this story to my kids. My son was very attentive to the story. At that time we lived on a busy street in the city of Coeur d'Alene, Idaho. Later, our Regional Fish and Game office started getting phone calls of an injured mule deer caught in a fence at the busy corner we lived on. The Regional Supervisor walked into my office and asked me if I knew anything of a wounded deer in front of my home on 15th street. No, I didn't know anything about it, but I silently wondered if my son had anything to do with it.

I went home a bit early and saw no deer. I asked our son if he knew anything. He explained he and a friend had stuck my mule deer mount across the street with its head peeking through a barbed wire fence and the rest was concealed by brush. When a passerby decided to take the mount home he rushed out and snatched it just as a cop pulled up and warned him he'd tell his dad if he put the deer head out again. Like father like son. So don't let your kids read this story; sorry I guess it's too late to warn you.

But It's Only a Toy

While Beth and the three children went to an Iowa grocery store, she noticed that our eight year old son had brought a toy along with him – a rubber garter snake. He played with the snake, wriggling it in front of his sisters and pretending that it was crawling along the shelves of canned goods. As Beth finished shopping and headed toward the checkout counter, she told our son to put the snake away so the checkout lady would not see it. "We might think it is a funny toy, but not everyone likes snakes, real or not," Beth said to the boy.

The rubber snake disappeared from sight and Beth and the kids stood in line at the cashier counter. Beth loaded the groceries onto the conveyer belt – canned goods, boxes of cereal and bags that held various produce items. As the checkout lady reached for the last bag of produce, she reached into the bag to see what items it contained and she pulled out the rubber snake. She dropped the toy and screamed at the same time. Everyone in the immediate area stopped what they were doing and stared at our little group.

Beth was speechless, our two daughters laughed and our son grabbed the snake. He looked around at everyone and said in a loud voice, "My mother told me to do it."

The Possum

The opossum is the only North American marsupial and in its native range is a close third to raccoons and skunks as a trouble maker. They are not very intelligent, but they are survivors having persisted for tens of thousands of years. We couldn't have a book of wildlife tales without at least mentioning brother possum.

The female opossum gives birth to hairless undeveloped young. After birth they find their way to the mothers pouch, grab onto a teat and stay there until they are fully developed. Opossum have an involuntary way of protecting themselves from some would be predators by feigning death.

When I was in high school an opossum wandered onto our back porch just as my stepfather, Bill, was opening the door to let his cat out. He was surprised to see the opossum and the opossum was surprised to see him. The opossum was so surprised it passed out and Bill thought he scared it to death. I told him the opossum would eventually wake up, but he didn't believe me and was certain it was dead. We watched the visitor for about a half an hour. It gradually woke from its deep sleep and waddled off to Bill's surprise. Bill was surprised the opossum came too and surprised I actually knew something.

My former roommate at Iowa State University, Clayton, sent me a picture of this rascal off his back porch. Seems he has been a local resident of his farm for several years. They're slow moving creatures, but very agile.

Picture 1. A well fed Iowa opossum.

45

The Great Hamster Breakout

After Beth and I moved from Iowa to Idaho, we bought an older home with a semi-finished basement. Beth and I slept in the basement bedroom (with its exposed heating ducts) while the kids had the three upstairs bedrooms.

As a family we always enjoyed pets. One year, our youngest daughter, Karin, had a pet hamster that gave birth to six babies and they grew rapidly. Their cage lid had a small hole at one end and we had covered it with masking tape. The hamsters could not reach the lid anyway because they were too short. At the other end of the cage was a small cardboard box with a door opening so the seven hamsters could hide in it. One night I was awakened by the pitter patter of tiny feet. I listened intently and discovered the noise came from the overhead heating duct. Were they rats? I thought. I woke Beth and whispered, "We have rats. Listen, you can hear them in the heating duct." Beth listened and heard the creatures moving through the heating ducts. "Oh no," she said and then hustled upstairs while I keyed in on the rats. In a minute, Beth was back down stairs and informed me that six of the seven hamsters had escaped during the night.

We needed to get them out of the heating system before they fell into the oil furnace and got smoked. I grabbed a screw driver and disconnected one end of the long pipe. While Beth held a box, I lowered the loose end. Flop, out came a dust covered hamster. We listened again heard more scurrying through the duct work. One found and five to go. I took apart another section of duct work and two more hamsters flopped into the box – three down and three more to find. With flashlights in hand, we started searching the rest of the house. I didn't think we'd ever find the rest. Ten minutes later, we found one under Karin's bed, another under our living room piano and the last racing across the dining room floor.

The hamsters were all returned to their cage and that's when we discovered how they escaped. The cardboard box had been pushed to the end of the cage with the taped hole in the wire lid. The hamsters climbed onto the box, chewed the tape, and one hamster evidently boosted the other six up to the hole to escape, until no one was left to help the last one. Evidently, these critters never heard of the US Marines who never leave another behind.

We secured the lid this time and finally went back to bed two hours after the start of the hunt. That morning our daughter was puzzled about two things – why were mom and dad so tired and how did three of her golden colored hamsters turn dark overnight.

Football Raccoon

Raccoons have honestly earned their reputation for being trouble makers. There is no doubt they cause home owners more problems than any creature in the woods. Although most of the time they cause us grief, they provide entertainment too.

A few years ago in late fall, our bird feeders on our veranda were emptied nightly by a family of four raccoons. The raccoons accessed the veranda, which is 16 feet off the ground, by climbing a nearby mountain maple tree. At first the raccoons were entertaining, but they became persistent pests. They tore the bird feeder apart and pulled the suet cage off its rack several times. We'd chase them away each night, but they'd always return. We refilled the bird feeder each day not only for the morning birds, but also for flying squirrels that would visit during the night when the raccoons were not around.

Picture 2. The raccoon family that visited our bird feeder and raised havoc.

Our two dogs, Daisy and Enrico, also loved to go out on the veranda to sniff around at night and watch birds during the day. However, at night we'd turn on a flood light and make sure the raccoons weren't at the feeder before we'd open a glass sliding door. Our concern was for the welfare of the dogs. An adult raccoon can create vet bills in an instant with one bite on a pet canine.

One autumn night, I turned on the light and looked around the veranda. I saw no creatures, so I slid the door open and let the dogs out. In less than a second, the dogs located a raccoon hiding under the gas grill. The challenge was on - dogs barking and trying to take a bite out of the raccoon and the raccoon snarling and snapping. I yelled, "Daisy, Rico, get in the house." Daisy, a female border collie, turned tail and ran back through the door way and into the house. Rico, a Catahoula leopard dog and lab mix, started backing up toward the door all the while growling and nipping with the snarling raccoon at his face. Rico backed up through the slider door into the room.

My worst fear was that the raccoon would follow the dog into the house and I would have to deal with an enraged raccoon. Well, that is what happened. As Rico passed by me, the raccoon was so focused on the dog it didn't notice me. It just so happened that I was wearing an over-stuffed pair of slippers shaped like a football (in Green Bay Packer green and gold of course). Without thinking, I took a swinging kick at the raccoon and caught it perfectly under its belly. The momentum lifted the raccoon six feet high into the air and it sailed twelve feet backward through the door. It hit the veranda deck with a flop and scurried off as I quickly slid shut the door. Wow! Too bad there wasn't a goal post. It was a perfect end over end kick. I immediately checked the dogs expecting to see half their faces missing. Neither dog had a scratch and we never saw the raccoon again.

Sweet Tooth Grizzly

An acquaintance told me a story a few years ago about a clever grizzly bear with a sweet tooth. We'll call the acquaintance Hal. Hal lived north of Priest River and had a shed in back of his house. For many years he kept his garbage in it. One day Hal discovered a grizzly bear had torn the shed apart for the garbage he kept in it. The grizzly kept returning expecting to find more garbage.

Hal had serious concerns if the grizzly was allowed to stay around any longer it may hurt someone, so he called IDFG to trap it and move it far away. Hal became frustrated when no one from IDFG responded. So Hal called IDFG again, but this time he asked how much a grizzly tag would cost because he was going to kill a grizzly bear. Hal got an instant response and was told what he already knew; that grizzly bears were protected, but was happy to hear someone would be out soon to trap it. A Conservation Officer set out a large culvert trap and baited it with donuts. Hal and a neighbor anxiously waited and watched, in the safety of Hal's home, for the grizzly to enter the trap and snatch a donut.

The grizzly eventually returned, smelled the tasty donuts, but instead of entering the trap it reached and stretched. It stretched its long front leg and with its paw and long claws it grabbed the donuts. It wolfed them down like there was no tomorrow. The trap was rebaited and the grizzly got another paw full of sweet yummy donuts. The trap wasn't working. Hal and his neighbor still worried that the grizzly would eventually cause someone serious injury, so they took things into their own hands. The neighbor had a black powder rifle and loaded it with large marbles. When the grizzly returned again it was shot in the butt with marbles and ran hell bent for leather and was never seen again.

We do not recommend anyone take the trapping or hazing of any protected, endangered or threatened species into their own hands. It should be left to professionals.

Snap Goes the Grackle

When I was in grade school a friend invited me to go channel catfishing with him and his dad. We fished a spot just above the Wilmot Dam on the Fox River of southeastern Wisconsin. After landing my first channel cat, I watched a grackle (a black bird) playing with the lures in a nearby fishermen's open tackle box. The bird became very excited when it discovered a rubber worm in a lower compartment. It struggled to pull it free. It finally succeeded, but soon had competition. Another grackle was watching and now that the work was done to free the rubber worm, the second bird tried to take it from its friend. The two birds struggled and fought over the worm as the fisherman was focused on his fishing. Then each bird secured one end of the rubber worm and started a tug of war. The worm stretched and stretched as far as a grackle could stretch it. Then to the surprise of both birds one of them lost its grip. The release of one end caused the rubber worm to snap back striking the winner in the head and bowling it over. The winner became frightened and flew off leaving the worm to the loser. That bird walked to the worm, picked it up and flew to a branch where it tried to eat what it thought was a tasty morsel. It soon tired of trying to eat the inedible rubber worm and flew back to the tackle box. The previously vanquished grackle then grabbed the worm and flew off with its prize.

The Great Chicken Roundup

While working for the Iowa Department Natural Resources (formerly Iowa Conservation Commission) Fisheries Bureau I was promoted and moved to an office near Manchester, in northeast Iowa. From time to time I was required to travel to Des Moines (three hours away) for work. One morning I was on my way to a staff meeting, driving toward an interstate to travel to Des Moines. I heard a travel advisory on the radio. Travel advisories were usually weather alerts for dangerous weather conditions. However, this traffic alert informed drivers to use caution on the interstate because a semi-tractor trailer carrying hundreds of chickens had flipped over. Most of the chickens were on the loose and causing traffic jams. The good news was the driver was unhurt.

Within minutes I was on my way south on the interstate and the accident came in view. There were cages strewn all over the median and some on the road. Most of the chickens had escaped from the cages during the accident. Some chickens weren't so lucky and were killed. However, there were hundreds of surviving chickens running to and fro with citizens and state troopers trying to catch them. There were chickens running into the corn and soy bean fields that paralleled the interstate and just plain dizzy chickens that walked in circles.

At first I thought I would be a good citizen and try to help roundup a chicken or two. I soon found the chickens were much more skilled at evading me than I was catching them. It wasn't long before a TV station field crew showed up with cameras in hand and a reporter with a microphone. That's when I looked at my watch and decided it was much more prudent for me to make my late morning meeting on time than to be seen on TV's evening news looking the fool trying to catch an elusive chicken.

You Have a Cougar In Your Garage

My friend Dave told me a funny mountain lion/cougar story that happened in the early 90s. Dave was a wildlife researcher with IDFG at the time and took a call about a cougar in a tree in an Avondale, Idaho, neighborhood. Dave and a colleague responded to the call. Upon reaching the scene, Dave and his partner slowly approached the huge cat and with one shot Dave put a tranquilizer dart into its rump. The cat immediately jumped out of the tree and ran as the two biologists gave chase. They knew the lion couldn't go far because Dave had made a good shot with the dart. A crowd gathered behind them and followed closely. They eventually found the lion in an open garage at a nearby house. The lion was lying down on the garage floor and almost fully tranquilized. At that same time a TV crew also joined the crowd.

Just as one of the biologists started to knock on the door of the homeowner to notify her of this situation, a woman came out the front door of the house. She saw the crowd and TV crew and asked what was going on. Dave responded, "You have a cougar in your garage." The lady stared at Dave and slowly shook her head as she retorted, "No it isn't a Cougar, it's a 1991 Chevy Impala." Dave just said, "Okay." The woman turned and walked back into the house. By then, the cat was asleep and the cougar team placed it in a large cage as the crowd and TV cameras watched. The cougar was safely transported into the nearby Panhandle National Forest and released unharmed. To this day the woman probably doesn't know that for a short time she had both a cougar and an Impala in her garage.

Ma Whitetail Doesn't Believe Dr. Spock

Back in the 70s the famous Dr. Spock professed disciplining children with a smack on the butt was entirely the wrong way to handle disobedience.

My friend Larry told me a story about a mother deer that had a method of discipline contrary to Dr. Spock. Many years ago he was archery hunting with his family. As they worked their way down a wooded ridge they had great vision of a field below. After a short time they came upon six whitetail deer grazing in the field; two does and four fawns. As they watched the game animals they saw the two does and three of the fawns walk to the edge of the woods below the field. One unsuspecting fawn was still grazing when it was left behind. After a few moments the lone fawn noticed the rest of the herd had left it on its own. The fawn was confused not knowing what direction they had gone. It did a tail spin that turned into a continuous whirl. Finally it noticed mother deer in the woods and ran hell bent for leather to her. It ran so fast it couldn't stop in time and smashed right into mom's butt knocking her over. The doe was visibly upset and after she righted herself she reared up and smacked the fawn on the nose knocking it down. I'm sure that fawn was much more attentive after that. As for Larry and his family, they spent most of the afternoon with laughing at the scene they had witnessed.

Just a note – it is also common for black and grizzly bear sows to discipline their cubs with a smack when they don't respond to orders.

The Air Borne Wood Chuck

I shouldn't have been surprised when I heard a story about a tree climbing marmot which reminded me of the woodchucks I watched in trees when I lived in the Midwest. Recently, Beth and I were told a story by my friend Tina that happened when she lived in Michigan. She and her husband were on one of their favorite woodland hiking trails. Without warning a burly woodchuck fell out of a tree onto Tina's shoulder. The woodchuck likely weighed about six pounds so it would have hit her with some impact. The clumsy critter careened off her shoulder onto the ground. It righted itself up and looked at her and ran with fear in one direction while Tina did the same in the opposite direction. I never knew woodchucks to have the tree hopping skills of a squirrel and this one certainly was no exception.

Don't Shoot

Shooting from a car or a roadway in many states, besides being dangerous, is illegal. One of the tools used by IDFG Conservation Officers to apprehend would be violators is the Animated Simulated Animal (ASA). Usually, an ASA is a full mount of a whitetail deer buck that has robotic ears, tail and neck. This allows the officer to give life like animation to the animal by controlling some movement. The ASA is placed in a conspicuous location within shooting range of a road while the officer waits in safe concealment. A violator breaks the law if they shoot even once from the road while the true sportsman gets out of the vehicle and walks off the roadway. To prevent any damage to the ASA, the game officer will call out to the true sportsman to not shoot.

As the story goes two IDFG Conservation Officers set up an ASA in an area where shooting from the roadway was a common occurrence. The morning started out uneventful while a heavy fog rolled in. The ASA was still visible through the fog, but there was an eerie ambiance to the surroundings. One Conservation Officer waited in a well concealed truck while the second officer hid in the nearby fog shrouded woods, within shouting distance of the road. A truck slowly pulled up and a hunter slinked his way out of the truck and off the road. In the thick fog he could still see the ASA. He approached the edge of the woods and drew his rifle up with the intent to make a legal shot. The Conservation Officer stood up from behind the hunter and shouted, "Don't shoot."

The startled hunter looked to the fog enveloped sky and said, "Is that you God?" The officer did not disturb the mood of the hunter's spiritual encounter. The hunter humbly walked back to the truck and drove off. The officer could not control his emotions and laughed so hard that tears ran down his cheeks.

The House Ermine

Ermine can become habituated to humans to the point they will tolerate even living with them. This story comes from Gordy and Tina. They live in an older home and have mice from time to time. While Tina and Gordy watched television one afternoon, an ermine popped up among some items on the floor. The little weasel seemed unafraid of them and snooped around a bit before leaving. Gordy and Tina expected that it would find its way out the same way that it came in. The ermine became a more frequent visitor.

One day Gordy heard a noise coming from a location where he had set a mouse trap only moments before. His first concern was thinking that the ermine was caught in the trap, but to his relief the ermine wasn't trapped, but had grabbed a mouse caught in the trap. The ermine could not pull the dead mouse from the trap, so Gordy pulled the trap from the ermine and removed the mouse. The ermine ran off and then just as quickly reappeared, so Gordy flipped the mouse to the ermine and it took the rodent. Since then Gordy and Tina have left the mouse removal to the ermine and have seen it doing its job in the house from time to time. As for the mice – what mice?

Daisy Gets a Pardon

We have a 12 x 8 foot garden pond in back of our house. In the pond are cattails, pond lilies and goldfish. The pond has a rubber liner and around the perimeter are large rocks and semi-aquatic plants. Beyond the pond edges and the perimeter rocks was Beth's perennial flower garden. Our border collie, Daisy, is not only a very smart dog, but she loves water. On hot days and even not so hot days, when we let her outside, she'll often bolt to the pond and dive in. Beth often caught Daisy in the pond and when Daisy exited the pond, the old dog would climb over the perimeter rocks and step across the flowers. To keep Daisy out of the pond I bought her a plastic kids wading pool, but I didn't get it out soon enough one spring, so when warm weather came Daisy headed to the pond.

One afternoon when Beth came home from work, she saw the pond rocks rolled onto the blooming flowers. Beth scolded Daisy for purportedly knocking rocks around and stomping on her flowers. Beth turned to me and said, "You better watch your Daisy dog. She has been into the pond again." Why none of the blame reached Enrico I don't know, but he sometimes jumps into the pond too, but not as much as Daisy.

About a week later I was sitting home at my computer and the dogs were in the house. Dogs have this extra sense of knowing when something or someone is outside near the house. Both dogs were relaxing on the floor near me when they jumped up and ran to the sliding door in the kitchen. They were barking excitedly. Usually it's a deer they are barking at. This time I followed them to the door and there in the garden pond was a wild animal. I grabbed my video camera and recorded the culprit for about five minutes. It was feasting on the cattails and other plants in the pond. It finally tired of the cattails and climbed out knocking rocks into the pond and stomping on Beth's flowers.

That afternoon when Beth returned from work I showed her the recording and Daisy got her pardon. In the video was a cow moose knocking rocks into the pond and crushing the once beautiful flowers.

Post script: Beth gave up trying to keep the colorful flowers growing around the pond. Now there is an area of colorful landscaping gravel in that border. If you can't beat them, join them.

Picture 3. Daisy watching a red squirrel eat sunflower seeds.

Exploding Elk

From time to time IDFG conservation officers get calls that no one else would want to see. Of all the IDFG personnel, the officers have the most responsibility, danger, adventure and range of duties. One morning two of our veteran agents Wayne and Jack received a call about a large dead animal in the water below the Post Falls Dam. It was lodged in a pile of brush at the boat ramp. It must have been in the river for weeks and the odor from the rotting animal caused a stir. The officers showed up shortly after the phone call and made an assessment. Stuck in a watery pile of brush was an absolutely rotten bloated cow elk. How it died they didn't know, but they had a scheme to remove it.

The two officers put down the tail gate of the work truck and one of them backed the truck into the water. When the tail gate was under water, the driver stopped the vehicle. With the help of a few other men, ropes and prods, the officers pushed, pulled and slid the rotten elk into the truck bed. Wayne slowly drove the truck up out of the water and up the boat ramp. Success, the slimy elk stayed in the open bed and Wayne was off to the county land fill to properly dispose of it. Jack followed in a second vehicle

Wayne proceeded to drive through town. However, as he rounded a corner, the elk slowly slid to the back of the truck bed. Wayne stopped for a stoplight and as he started forward on a green light, the elk slid out, hit the pavement with a loud ka-wumph and exploded behind him. Jack immediately called Wayne on the Fish and Game radio and told him he just lost his passenger. Wayne looked in his rear view mirror and there in the middle of the intersection was a giant amorphous blob. He slowed to a stop. The weight and momentum of the water logged carcass carried the dead animal off his truck bed. Now what to do?

Traffic was in a bit of a snarl so the police were summoned and then a city crew brought in an end loader. It was soon evident one end loader wasn't going to do the job. The giant blob just slid along the road as the single end loader tried to scoop it up. A second end loader was brought in and the two end loaders faced each other and scooped the mess up. After the large chunks were removed crews with shovels cleaned what was left. All the while, the stench of the rotten elk was spreading the entire width and length of the disaster. Now what to about the stench permeating through town? The fire department was called in to hose down the street and flush the remaining mess into the sewer system. The sewer water drains into the Spokane River. Anyone interested in a swim? Oh yes, the big chunks were hauled to the county land fill with the tail gate up this time and the entire truck cleaned at an auto wash.

SCARY SITUATIONS

Muskie Bite

A late friend Steve was a highly regarded research scientist with the Wisconsin Department of Natural Resources. One of Steve's studies, in the late 70s, was assessing the stocking of fingerling musky in local lakes. He and his wife were avid snorkelers. On a warm summer afternoon, Steve and his wife decided it may be a good day to cool off and enjoy some recreational snorkeling in a local lake that, by the way, he had his musky study on. They rowed into several scenic secluded bays and enjoyed the summer day. After snorkeling at their favorite spots there was one more gorgeous bay they wanted to try. They anchored their small boat, dropped into the cool water and enjoyed the remainder of the afternoon. Steve swam to the stern of the boat and was about to catapult himself in when he felt something grab his foot. A split second later he felt the pain of dozens of teeth. He struggled to kick the predator off his foot. After several kicks the predator released. Steve lifted himself into the boat. His foot was bleeding profusely with dozens of teeth marks and lacerations. After a visit to the hospital with treatment and stitches some of his friends decided to measure the width of the bite. From what was visible it was estimated the musky to be in the 25 to 30 pound class or 46 to 50 inches in length. My friend went back out snorkeling as soon as the doctor gave him the okay.

Lau Lau — The Man Killer

Fishing for big catfish is my favorite fishing pastime. On a recent trip to Guyana, South America. I fished for several large catfish including the redtail, jau, and lau lau. The largest and most storied is the lau lau which has purportedly attacked and consumed humans. There is a picture on the internet of a lau lau that has a man partially down its throat. The picture does have some uncertainty since some believe it has been photo shopped. After fishing for them and catching one of 80 inches in length and nearly 200 pounds I believe it is possible.

The guides we had in Guyana were all natives, very well-mannered and knowledgeable about fishing. One of my favorite guides was Roger. He was in his late 40s and of African descent. He told me his great grandparents had been slaves and after being freed they assimilated into the native tribes. I asked him if he had any good lau lau stories and he did. He told me of a fish he had caught, when he was in his late teens that was about 130 inches in length, he released the fish after measuring it.

The second story he told was terrifying and happened when he was a youngster. A common summer practice of the children in all of the villages is to swim in the rivers on hot days. On a warm summer afternoon a half a dozen children or more gathered at the local swimming hole and were enjoying the afternoon. The hole was next to a cut bank near deep water which allowed the kids to dive into the clear water off the bank. They played and splashed water making a great commotion. All but one of the kids was on the bank awaiting a chance to jump into the pool leaving one boy in the water. The boy dove underwater and swam along the bottom perhaps looking for fish or clams. Out of the deep darker water swam up a giant lau lau. The kids on the bank screamed and screamed to alert the lone swimmer, but he couldn't hear them. The monster lau lau grabbed the unsuspecting boy and drug him back into the deep water and he was never seen again. After coming to know more of the lau lau I believe his story.

Jungle Camping

In 2017 I went to Guyana in South America for a 10 day jungle camping and fishing trip. It was an exciting adventure packed trip with many new experiences. Each fisherman was set up with an 8 x 8 walled tent with sheets and an air mattress. By my standards they were comfortable conditions. The guides had separate accommodations and slept in hammocks with only a large canopy above them. Like many camping adventures it rained every day.

All of the fishing guests were cautioned to check sheets, clothing and tent corners every night for scorpions, spiders, snakes or any other creatures that could inflict a serious bite or sting. Everyday an attendant entered each tent to change out towels, sheets and make the bed. My only complaint was that the zippers on the tents were never fully closed after the attendant left. Every evening I did my best to check for creatures and made sure all zippers were closed. One evening I inspected the edge of my tent door and there was a large 2-inch diameter hairy brown spider. I flicked it into the jungle. The next morning I met my fishing companions at breakfast and I told the story of my spider encounter. Another fisherman said he had a story too. He said, "I crawled into my bed last night and I was about to fall asleep when I felt something crawling on my chest. In the dark I cautiously brushed it off then turned on a flashlight and saw it was a large harmless cricket. Thinking it was no threat to me I let the cricket go. A few moments later as I was about to fall asleep, I again felt something crawling on my chest. I thought it was the cricket so I flicked it off my chest. This time when I shined the light on the critter, it was a large dark hairy spider; a red wood spider. I took my shoe and flattened it." I liked his story much better than mine.

At dusk, many different species of bats flew around. They'd dart here and there and just miss collisions with us. Most bats were searching for insects. None of the fisherman were troubled by the bats, but one night a native guide found a vampire bat on his left shoulder. He immediately knocked it off and saw it had drawn blood. Two nights later he found a second bat on the same shoulder. How unlucky can you get to find a vampire bat sucking blood from you not once, but twice during a week?

Man Bait

In 2008, Beth and I took a trip to Europe which included a four-day stay in Barcelona. I always try to take advantage any opportunity to fish while traveling. I hired a guide to fish for the famous Wels catfish on the River Ebro. The Wels was illegally introduced into the River Ebro in the early 70s and now fish exceeding 200 pounds are caught. Like the Lau Lau, this catfish has also been known to attack and eat humans. The guide helped me hook an 82 pound Wels on my first afternoon and five more the next morning. It was a fantastic fishing expedition.

My guide also had several bank fishermen that he set up before he met me. He told me one of his fishermen was lucky to be alive. He explained two of his clients were bank fishing when one hooked into a monster Wels. In order to better manage reeling in the behemoth he waded into the water to his waist. As the angler was winning the battle, the fished turned to him and in a rush grabbed him by the thigh and started to drag him into deeper water. Upon seeing his fishing partner in need of dire help, the other fisherman rushed over and grabbed his companion and pulled him to the safety of the shore. If you examine pictures 4 and 5 you can see the immense gape on the mouth of a Wels catfish. A fish of 125 to 200 pounds could swallow a small human.

Picture 4. Vaughn with an 82 pound Wels catfish on the Ebro, Catalonia, Spain.

Picture 5. The 12 or more inch gape of an 82 pound Wels catfish. A 200 pound Wels could easily swallow a small human.

Teddy the Troublesome Brown Bear

Several months before graduation from Iowa State University I applied for a technician position with Alaska Department of Fish and Game (ADFG). To my delight I got the position and in May 1969 I graduated and flew to Kodiak, Alaska. Alaska and Kodiak Island were everything I thought they would be. Every day was an adventure and it was an exciting place to live. Pete, another technician, and I stayed in a comfortable cabin on the Karluk River on Kodiak National Wildlife Refuge. The cabin had a large dining/kitchen/living room and a comfortable bunk room with a back door. The main entry into the cabin was a screen door that opened to a small boot room separated from the living area by a wooden door

Pete and I were responsible for managing a salmon weir (fence-like structure to control movement of salmon) on the Karluk River. The sockeye salmon numbers began to increase as we entered the spawning season and so did the numbers of brown bears on the river. My first encounter with a brown bear was with a brute I named Bruno. I was fishing Karluk Lake for Arctic Char and noticed a big bear perhaps half a mile away at the mouth of Spring Creek, a tributary to Karluk Lake. I grabbed my camera and headed that way. I slowly walked up Spring Creek and before long I saw Bruno walking downstream toward me. He was searching for salmon methodically looking left and right as he progressed and didn't see me. Suddenly he caught my scent, looked up, spun to his right and ran up the stream bank to his right. I went the opposite direction and decided I couldn't take any more excitement.

I saw Bruno several more times and we eventually named seventeen bears we saw, including a sub-adult we named Teddy. Despite all of the bears roaming near our cabin, sleeping was never a problem, until one morning about 0300 Pete whispered, "Vaughn, Vaughn, there's a bear on the porch."

I said, "What"?

He repeated, "There's a bear on the porch." I got up, grabbed a flash light and headed to our front door which led to the porch. The door was open so I slowly approached, then with my flashlight, carefully peered into the passageway. There indeed was a brown bear rooting through a garbage can. I slammed the door shut and the bear scrambled out the door just as I locked it. It was obvious what caused the brown bear to get into the porch. Previously, we kept the garbage in the kitchen, but Pete was troubled by the odor, so that night he moved the garbage to the porch. The attraction of a free meal brought the bear right back. The bear came back and I chased it off again and again by shouting. The last time it came back we were both in for a surprise. Pete had an idea of climbing up a ladder just outside our back door to the roof. Previously we set the ladder up to watch bears from the roof. Pete climbed to the roof while I went to a nearby window with my camera. My thought was not to take a picture, but to frighten the bear with the cameras flash. The brown bear saw me, walked to the window and peered in at me. I took my camera and clicked. The light flashed in its face. I blinded myself with the reflection of the flash off the window. I startled the bear and made it dizzy. However, I thought I was going to die at the paws of an enraged brown bear. I stumbled around for our .338 Winchester Magnum rifle, but couldn't locate it. The bear stumbled off. Little did I know I had taken a picture – a night portrait of Teddy.

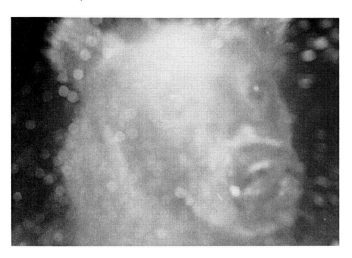

Picture 6. Portrait of Teddy Bear, through our kitchen window, on the first night he caused trouble. He was later described as a typical irresponsible carefree sub-adult brown bear.

A basic mistake was made that lured the brown bear to our cabin. Pete had moved our garbage can to the porch and the brown bear naturally was attracted to it. It was now conditioned to associate our cabin with food. I reported the event during our evening radio check to the fish station in

Kodiak. The agent neglected to pass my story on to the federal wildlife service refuge manager who needed to know about bear problems. Teddy continued to be a mischievous bear getting in our way all the time. It got into our weir chasing fish, it destroyed our rubber raft, and at night he walked endlessly around our cabin- moaning and wearing a path around it. One morning I woke up and Teddy was peering through a window at me. Since I continued to report this dangerous situation with this brown bear, I expected the US Fish and Wildlife Service to fly out to us, dart the nuisance bear and haul him off. Nobody responded.

Teddy continued destroying equipment and property. It all came to an head one evening just as Pete and I finished supper. We heard a crashing sound from a window in the SW corner of our main room. It was Teddy smashing in the glass. I shouted at the bear, "Teddy get the hell out of here," as I held the .338. Pete scrambled for my 7mm Remington magnum. I yelled again and again. To scare Teddy, I shot a round through the wall above the brown bear. That only infuriated the brown bear as it snarled and moved to the next window - which was located above our kitchen table. The bear snarled and ripped away the window screen, then slammed into the window frame and sent it skidding across our kitchen table. The window frame landed at my feet without breaking a pane of glass. I shouted louder. Teddy's jaws were popping; the sign of an enraged bear. Then he started to climb in through the open space placing his front paws on our kitchen table. As the brown bear catapulted itself in, his hind feet reached the window sill. There was no more time for patience. I aimed at its chest and the blast from the gun knocked the brown bear back outside. The 225 grain bullet delivered a mortal wound through the chest, passed through a lung and broke the spine. As it dragged itself off, Pete put another round in it. The dangerous brown bear was dead.

Later, over the radio, I reported the incident to our supervisor. I said, "We had a bear incident this evening. What should I do with the body?"

The supervisor freaked out. "Body? What body? What happened to Pete?"

"No, Pete's okay, I had to kill that bear I reported two weeks ago." After I gave the details I was instructed to write a report for the local conservation officer. After that everybody and their brother had to come to Kodiak Island to see the dead bear. Pete and I thought we were in trouble with ADFG; that our careers were over because of the bear killing. The officer flew to our outpost and read my report.

Picture 7. Teddy Bear lies outside the field cabin where he died. You can see the damage to the cabin in the background; a shattered window far right and torn screen and missing window over the kitchen table at left.

"Why the hell did you wait so long?" he yelled at me. I explained I reported the bear incident the same night, I reported the continuous problems and the shooting the same night. He stared at me and said, "Why did you wait so long to kill it?" It was a sad case where communication breaks down and the people that could have saved this bear ignored our repeated requests for relocating the bear.

Bear Bait

Bear encounters in Alaska are not uncommon. There's seldom any conflict when a condition of mutual respect is present. But that isn't always the case, especially with hungry old bears in the fall or a sow with cubs.

Jason, a family friend, went to Alaska with his dad to hunt moose and brown bear with an uncle who was a resident Alaskan. On one crisp autumn morning, Jason ventured away from his family with the intent to harvest a moose with his bow. Jason was also armed with a knife and a hand gun. As he quietly worked his way down a game trail through a maze of alders and brush, he spotted a lone brown bear a short distance away. Jason had no intention of harvesting a brown bear with his bow, so he gave the brown bear ample room. Jason slowly started to back away from the big bear. The bear scented Jason and watched him as he tried to escape from the bear's territory. Without provocation, the brown bear took off in pursuit of Jason. Jason turned and ran for the safety of more substantial fire power than a handgun, knife or bow. As he ran full speed down the trail he yelled, "Bear, bear, bear." Jason cast his bow aside to lighten his load and knew he'd never have time to draw his hand gun, so he kept running and yelling. He finally sighted his dad and uncle. The swift brown bear substantially closed the distance between them. His dad and uncle heard the commotion and were ready to help immediately. Both men fired several rounds killing the predator. The bear was tagged and to this day Jason and his family don't have any idea why this unprovoked brown bear decided it would go after a human.

Brown Bear

Matt, an Alaskan friend of mine, looks forward to his annual two week moose hunt and stay in the family cabin. The cabin is located on a large island surrounded on all sides by the Tanana River and is in prime moose country. Matt told me his favorite way to hunt moose is from a canoe. He paddles from one backwater area to another and into large beaver ponds. In the fall, the water is usually low and cold and his hunt very leisure.

On one crisp morning, Matt was enjoying the moment. He stopped occasionally to search for moose by glassing the water ahead and nearby hillsides with binoculars. From time to time he saw brown bears. He'd usually see them first and give them plenty of space, but kept his rifle close. Then, without warning, an unprovoked brown bear burst out of the nearby willows and charged him. The water was shallow and the brown bear easily crossed the short distance rapidly. Matt dropped the paddle and reached for his rifle. The brown bear was now so close he could hear him breathing. Matt knew he wouldn't have the time to get off a shot and he'd likely be mauled by the brown bear. To Matt's surprise the brown bear turned at the last moment and ran back into the willows. It was Matt's fortune that he just experienced what is known as a false charge.

Algonquin Surprise

One year we took our family on a two week camping trip on a tour of the Great Lakes. Our plan was to circle around the lower lakes in the U.S. and then go north from Niagara Falls and west through Canada. We heard Algonquin Provincial Park was beautiful and planned to spend several days there. Our stay in Algonquin was fun packed with fishing, sightseeing, catching frogs, evening camp fires and s'mores. Our son and younger daughter decided to venture into the nearby woods and walk a trail while our elder daughter stayed with us and her dog. About ten minutes into their hike, the two explorers came running out of the woods yelling their heads off. Our young daughter, with a dozen hornets or more buzzing around her head and stinging her, ran to Beth who tried desperately to smack them off. Our son also had a dozen hornets swarming around him. He ran past us to an outhouse. The hornets followed him into the outhouse, but were left inside after he ran out and slammed the door shut. We all ran from the camp site and fortunately left the nasty insects behind.

Twenty minutes later, I returned to the camper and was hit in the head by a hornet. I ran again to get away from them. We waited a half hour more and I returned to found the area was safe. Both children had been stung about three times – each in the same places – on the same eyelid, the same place on their cheek and the same place on their neck. When the truth finally came out, the children explained what really happened. They saw a hornet fly into a hole on the ground and as kids will do, our son took his walking stick and proceeded to drill the hole out further. The hornets apparently did not want a larger entry way and made it known to the intruders. Unfortunately for another camper, we forgot about the hornets left in the outhouse. While we were all sitting around our fire ring an unsuspecting adult male camper decided he needed to use the outhouse. He opened the door and entered only to come flying out and screaming, "Hornets, hornets." Is there anyone out there who enjoys the outdoors and doesn't have a bee, wasp or hornet story?

Who You Gonna Call?

When I was a young hunter I was excited to learn how to call in game animals. Game calls come in a wide variety of shapes, sizes, and are made of a variety of materials. Some, like deer and elk calls, are essentially reed instruments while turkey calls are frequently small, open cedar boxes with a wood lever to stroke over the top to simulate the yelp of a hen turkey. Hunters practice on their game calls like a music student with an instrument. Game calling has become so popular that there are deer, elk and turkey calling contests. I pride myself on my game calling skills. However, the seasoned game caller will tell you that although you may be trying to call in a nice buck or a bull elk, you never know who you're gonna call.

While predator calling for coyotes and red fox, I've brought in great horned owls, hawks, deer, and bear. But my bet is one of the most surprised hunters was a young man from Bonners Ferry, Idaho. As the story goes, he was calling bull elk with a cow elk call early one morning. Shortly after he started calling he saw movement. He thought it may be an elk. He held his fire to be sure of his target and there to his surprise was a grizzly bear that responded to his cow calling. Before the bear got too close, the young man moved away from a dangerous situation.

Several years ago, my son was using a cow call to bring in a bull elk. He was concealed on the ground and hadn't been calling long when he saw something at a distance coming in very slowly. It finally came in close enough for him to see it was a mountain lion and it was stalking what the lion thought was a cow elk. My son stood up and the mountain lion ran off.

A friend of mine had a similar experience while calling turkey. He was sitting on the ground leaning back on a large tree. He was as still as a dead stick he said. He could barely hear something in back of the tree, so he gradually turned around the tree to see. There looking him straight in the eye was a mountain lion. From this point we don't know who was more surprised – my young friend or the lion that ran off. Either way, my friend left the woods – smart move.

Many years ago, a friend and I were celebrating New Year's Eve in a bar in northern Wisconsin. We were bored with the lack of other young people, so we decided to do some night calling for coyotes. It was an incredibly cold moonlit evening as we pushed through hip deep snow to a large marsh by the Wisconsin River. I used a dying rabbit call for about ten minutes without success. The bitter cold soon became unbearable, so we decided to go back to the bar. As we started to walk out, I noticed something very dark and very large running toward us. It was a large black bear. When the bear came within 30-40 yards of us it stopped, walked in a tight circle, sat on its rear and looked at us. We thought it was a good time to leave the hibernation confused bear. We walked backwards very briskly to my car. A few days later, we heard another report of a bear out of its den. It's unusual for a bear not to be in its den in January, but that does happen.

Jon and The Wolves

When I was a youngster my favorite story was Peter and the Wolf. The wolf in the story was a scary animal. Years later when the Federal Government reintroduced the gray wolf in the Northwest, the reintroduction was met with mixed opinions. As employees of the Idaho Department of Fish and Game (IDFG) Beth and I were to have a neutral position and explain the IDFG management plan.

Wolves were taking a foothold in north Idaho during the early 2000s and wolf-human encounters were starting to take place more frequently. Our son Jon is an avid archery elk hunter and he knows that some of the best places in north Idaho to find large branch antlered bulls are in drainages of the Coeur d'Alene Mountain Range. One morning, he headed deep into one of his favorite drainages. As a routine pack item, he carried a headlamp knowing that he'd be traveling back in the dark. Dusk approached and he started to head out of the woods. As he hiked out the trail, he heard faint footsteps in the woods. Someone or something was following him. Our son stopped and the noise would stop, he'd walk and the steps started again. The third time it happened he turned to cast his headlamp 360 degrees to see what was following him. There clearly at 20 yards were two wolves. He knew better than to run (running stimulates the chase response in predators), however he picked up his pace.

At one point the wolves split up and the hunter had one animal on either side flanking him. His concern was they would try to cut him off the trail. The wolves gradually became more daring getting closer and closer. After being followed or stalked by the wolves for over a mile our son finally reached his parked motorcycle. Once on the motorcycle he didn't waste any time getting back to camp and to safety. Wolves are very curious about people and their activities, but that does not mean they shouldn't be treated without a great deal of respect. Since that incident he and I always pack a handgun during the archery elk season.

CAN'T BE EXPLAINED

Great Grandma's Maggots

Words of caution; if you have a weak stomach do not read this story. I started fishing when I was about six years old and I remember an old timer telling me one of his tricks to success was to spit on his worm. The saliva was an apparent attractant and enticed the fish to take the bait. I used the technique and always thought

The following story takes the saliva technique to an extreme. My friend Dale told me the best fisherman he had ever known was his great grandma. She had an unusual way of preparing her bait and her favorite bait was fly maggots. Great grandma would hold a few of them in her mouth between her cheek and gum. She believed it kept them livelier and wiggled longer. One day great grandma forgot she had a maggot in her mouth and took a sip of coffee. Whoops!

In our modern day of scientific fishing there are many scents and sprays available to fisherman. So you don't need to risk the chance that you may swallow your maggots.

This Frog was Smart

Many families in southern Wisconsin can hardly wait for summer to go to the north woods of Wisconsin. Wisconsin has more than 8,000 lakes so fishing and boating are important past times. Here, vacationing families relax, hike, camp and fish. The lakes of northern Wisconsin are famous for musky fishing and for good reason muskies are called the fish of 10,000 casts. Ask any musky fisherman because the common issue each will have after a day of fishing is a sore shoulder. Not from catching fish, but from heaving huge lures all day.

One of the popular tourist attractions near Woodruff, Wisconsin was a place called Aqualand. It had a menagerie of wild and domestic animals. There were chickens that would play a few notes on a piano for a few grains of corn (cost a quarter), goats that would walk a tight rope and black bears that would guzzle a 12 ounce bottle of soda called bruin brew.

A popular attraction in Aqualand was a small pond loaded with 8 to 15 pound muskies. The gimmick at the musky pond was to buy a couple of leopard frogs at an outrageous price and flip them to the ravenous muskies. Typically the frog would hit the water and three to six muskies would race to it. The frog was safe until it moved and then it was first come first serve. One lucky musky would snatch it and the human viewers would cheer ooohs and ahhhs. I likened the experience to the Roman Coliseum where Christians were thrown to lions as the spectators cheered the excitement.

Everyone in our family looked forward to watching muskies at the musky pond especially my stepfather. One day my stepfather, all dressed in Sunday clothes, went to the musky pond. After feeding several frogs to the muskies, he flipped in a frog that must have been smarter than most. When this frog hit the water with a ska-ploosh, it floated motionlessly. Muskies raced to it, but the frog did not move. One by one the muskies grew tired of waiting for the frog to show life and the fish drifted away. That's when the frog would give a kick toward shore. The muskies raced to it, but the same thing would occur; the frog would lay motionless until the muskies left. Finally after repetitive strokes to shore the frog made it safely to the bank. My stepfather uttered some four letter words and retrieved the frog.

He pitched it back into the pond. This happened three or four times with the persistent frog reaching the safety of the bank each time.

Finally, my stepfather squatted down at the edge of the pond and before the frog could reach the bank he grabbed it by a front leg. Just as he was pulling the frog from the water a large musky raced to the bank, hit my stepfather's hand and simultaneously chomped down on the doomed frog. My stepfather slid down the muddy bank and part way into the water. His clean pants were soaked and muddy. He was furious as the crowd laughed at him and cheered for the musky. I had been rooting for the amphibian as I always cheer for the underfrog.

Pronghorn Roundabout

In 1987 my late brother David Mark Gibson and I were on a trip to hunt and fish in Montana and South Dakota. After a successful mule deer hunt and fishing in Montana we were on our way through Wyoming to South Dakota. David had never seen a live pronghorn before so when I spotted a herd of pronghorn just off the road in Wyoming I slowed my 1979 Jeep Cherokee. As usual when I slowed from high to low speed it backfired. The backfire terrified the herd of pronghorn, after all it was hunting season. They ran as fast as they could around a big hill. Circling the hill only brought them back toward us. Seeing us, the animals ran back around the hill to get away only to return again and then follow the same path around the hill.

We decided since we were just seeing the same running pronghorn over and over it was in our and their best interest if we moved on. However, we did a lot of laughing about the poor herd of pronghorn that as hard as they ran just kept running back to us.

Card Shark Brown Bear

I learned living in Alaska's bush meant you listened to the radio and played cards at night or you were bored out of your mind. So playing cards, listening to Wolf Man Jack and telling stories at night were favorite pastimes. One of the stories that came out of the Karluk Lake field station where I was stationed was about a brown bear that apparently had a penchant for watching the technicians play cards in the evening.

One evening the brown bear was watching through a kitchen window while the card players sat at a table nearby. As the brown bear watched unnoticed, the betting was intense and the winner's pot was growing. The brown bear apparently wanted to point at a card it wanted a player to discard, but forgot about the glass window. It placed its paw on the window pane and the weight of its paw broke the glass. The brown bear's paw fell onto the shoulder of a card player and the broken glass fell all around the table. Everyone was stunned by the surprise visitor. The card players stayed motionless, including the player with the huge paw on his shoulder. The brown bear gently withdrew his paw and walked off into the dark. Anyone ready for a game of cards – brown bear style?

Authors note: the brown bear and grizzly bear are the same bear. The bear is called a brown bear along coastal Alaska and British Columbia because it is darker than the interior bear often called the grizzly bear because of its grayish or "grizzled" look.

The Stalking Bear

For more than fifteen years, our family kept three horses. Two of them were rescue horses. We were fortunate to have a very kind neighbor who let us pasture them in his 40 acre field for several months each year. The grassy field near our home had a couple acres of timber. That field was next to a much larger timbered property and we were always concerned about cougars and bears bothering the horses.

One late summer afternoon we were on our way to town and stopped by the pasture to check on our small herd of three equines. We noticed a black bear putting on an apparent stalk of our horses. The horses were grazing near a few shade trees in the north east corner. Horses by nature are very alert, except for my old half-blind Appaloosa. The other two horses were watching the bear warily. I said to Beth, "I think we have trouble."

I expected the threatening bruin to pursue and tackle one of our critters for lunch. The bear came within 40 yards of the horses. Suddenly, the two younger horses put on a sprint, not an escape move, but toward the black bear. The black bear froze for a moment and then burst in a full gallop for the opposite fence line. The horses came within a few feet of running the terrified bear over. I was dumbfounded; I saw a sight I didn't expect to see.

Several weeks later, I saw perhaps the same black bear in an apple tree in the horse pasture. The two speedsters were there waiting for the bear to come down, perhaps to give chase again. Likely all the bear wanted to do was feast on apples, not horse meat.

Picture 8. A black bear on the prowl for apples.

Buddha Bear

Another bear story with our three horses happened in our yard one autumn day. When summer was over each year, we would bring the horses from the neighbor's pasture a half mile away to our property. We had two corral sections fenced off that totaled about one-half acre. The two sections were separated for the most part by a grassy area that was our drainage field, but the two sections were connected on one end by a fenced passage way that allowed the horses to move from one section to the other. When I wanted the horses to stay in the upper section, I just closed a gate in the passage way to prevent them from coming down to the corral section by the barn.

One day, Vaughn and I were in the kitchen when I looked out our window and noticed one of the horses pacing back and forth along the fencing that separated the upper wooded horse section from the drainage field. The other two horses were standing close to the closed gate. The first horse kept pacing the entire length of the corral section and staring into a small stand of trees. I pulled out my binoculars and focused them onto the area in the trees. I could not believe my eyes. I passed the binoculars to Vaughn. Sitting like a big brown Buddha between two trees was the largest black bear that we had ever seen. It was just sitting there, ignoring the horses and evidently everything else. Now I understood why the horses were agitated. I also knew that someone had to go out to the upper section and open the gate so the three horses could put some distance between themselves and the bear that was only 50 feet away from them.

I turned to Vaughn to ask him to go out and open the gate when he said, "I'll get my gun to cover you when you open that gate." He brought his rifle to the kitchen porch and held it as he also tried to juggle a movie camera to film what was about to happen. I slowly made my way into the first corral and then walked toward the passage way gate all the while keeping the bear in view. The bear just sat there. I edged up to the gate and opened it. The horses ran down the alley way to the corral in front of the barn. I quickly followed them. The bear just sat there. As I exited the lower corral, I decided to watch the bear from there. Now I wished that I had thought to bring my camera. The bear just sat there.

I called to Vaughn to come closer, where I was standing, to get a better view of the bear with his movie camera. He stayed on the kitchen deck and said that he could see just fine. The bear just sat there. Later the bear left without causing any problems. We never saw it again.

This Dog's Best Friend

I have never heard of a dog and a wild black bear getting along and enjoying each other's company. So this story had to be in this book. Friends Gordy and Tina live in the woods near Kellogg, Idaho and their property is surrounded by U.S. Forest Service land. One afternoon Gordy and Tina heard their dog barking. It usually barked to alert them when someone was in the yard. When they checked to see what the commotion was about, they saw an adult black bear. The bear tired of the barking dog and walked back into the woods.

The bear eventually returned, but this time the encounter between their dog and the black bear was different. The two former adversaries developed a playful relationship chasing each other around in the yard playing animal tag. The two became summer pals. The bear returned numerous times and the two had a fun summer. The bear never became a problem.

Pie Loving Bruin

My friend Bart told me a story of a bear he knew as a little boy. Sixty years ago Bart grew up on a large family ranch near White Bird, Idaho. He referred to the men working the ranch as "the cowboys." The cowboys hunted game from time to time for food for the ranch hands. One spring they killed a bear for food and soon found out it had a cub. The cub was brought back to the ranch, raised and became conditioned to people showing no fear or aggression to the family. Bart said the bear was a sow and she just kept growing. He and the other kids on the ranch played with it like it was a pet. They wrestled with it and the bear rolled the kids around and despite the rough housing, the bear was always playful and never hurt anyone.

Bart said his grandmother made great mince meat pies and from time to time the pies would disappear before she could get them on the table. The thief was finally discovered when she caught the bear stealing one of her pies. Grandmother was only 4 foot 9 inches tall, but when she caught the bear with the pie, she grabbed a broom and chased it through the house swatting it whenever she got within range. Granny was so upset she said the bear had to go. The bear was loaded onto a truck and hauled off many miles away and released.

Later that year, the time when bears go into hibernation, the family discovered the door to the basement fruit cellar was busted to pieces. As they were about to repair the door, they found the bear inside the fruit cellar - fast asleep for the long winter. The door was repaired and the bear left to sleep through winter. From time to time stored produce was retrieved and the bear was never disturbed. Bart also said the bear snored so loud it could be heard under the floor of the house. For the next 6 years the bear would return late in the year to hibernate in the fruit cellar then leave in spring. Its snoring marked the beginning and end of hibernation. Bart said there was only one person on the ranch that snored louder than the bear and that was his petite grandmother.

The authors do not recommend nor endorse handling wildlife and advise that wild animals should never be considered in the same light as domestic animals. Young wild animals should never be disturbed or kidnapped from their mother. Wild animals should not be pets, there are laws to prevent citizens from keeping wildlife. If you see a young or injured wild animal, please contact a fish and game office, law enforcement, animal control or a natural resource agency for help.

The Genius Fox Squirrel

When we lived in rural northeast Iowa, we had an abundance of fox squirrels and a few grey. Each autumn I would try to come up with an ingenious way to feed the birds, but keep squirrels out of the feeder. Time and time again I would fail. Within a day, the squirrels would figure out my new strategy.

A neighbor of ours, I'll call Ed, invented an electric squirrel proof feeder. It also worked on large birds like blue jays. Ed made a large bird feeder with several uninsulated rings of copper wire around the feeder. He'd watch the feeder from the comfort of his living room. When a squirrel or blue jay came to the feeder he'd plug the other end into his house 110 outlet. The jay or squirrel would get lit up like a giant stadium bulb and go flying off the feeder. The only problem was you had to be watching the feeder to select the culprit and not a desirable cardinal, nuthatch or grosbeak. (I knew that if I was to make one, our son would prank one of his sisters into checking the electrified feeder and send her screaming.)

After considerably more thought about a squirrel proof bird feeder, I had an idea. I cut two holes in a plastic gallon milk jug, tied 3-feet of fishing line to the jug and then filled it with sunflower seeds. Then I suspended the jug from a tree branch which was at least five feet off the ground. The squirrels could not reach my invention from the tree or the ground. At last success!

Nope, after two days there was a fox squirrel inside the milk jug. How was this squirrel getting in? With movie camera in hand I watched one morning. Mr. Fox Squirrel came skipping along the ground, climbed the tree and crawled out on the branch. With its hind feet hanging onto the branch, the squirrel grabbed the line with its front feet and patiently pulled the string up (with the weight of the seed in the jug). After hand lining the jug within inches of its nose, the squirrel swung the jug up and with one fluid movement released its hind feet from the branch and in mid-air dove headfirst into the hole in the jug. As the jug was falling, the squirrel pulled the rest of itself into the jug. With the added weight of the squirrel, the jug bounced mid-air several times. Once the jug settled it gorged on the sunflower seeds (I have a movie of this fox squirrel). When the squirrel was satisfied, it jumped to the ground and ran off.

I gave up trying to trick fox squirrels to keep them from the bird seed. They obviously have a higher IQ.

The Creative Pine Squirrel

My friend Greg told me a story of a pine squirrel that started thinking outside of the box. (Pine squirrels are also called red squirrels). Greg has a bird-feeder on his deck that also became an attractant for an innovative pine squirrel. At first Greg thought it was odd that this squirrel brought a Douglas fir cone to the feeder every time it came to feed. The squirrel left the cone in the trough of the feeder where the sunflower seeds were stored.

Over time Greg noticed that the seed trough became so stuffed with cones that the birds could no longer get to the seeds. The squirrel would return to the feeder, remove a cone or two and feast on the sunflower seeds. Then the squirrel replaced the cones back into the trough. Greg removed a few of the cones to open an area where the birds could feed and within a day or two the squirrel had it plugged with cones again, keeping all of the sunflower seeds for its own use.

Troublesome Chipmunks

Chipmunks are cute to watch, but they can create serious issues with vehicles when they use them as a home. Typically, rodents will venture through any opening they can find exploring for a safe place to build a nest. One chipmunk met his demise by venturing too far into the air conditioning system in our 2005 Ford Expedition. It got trapped and died. That was the most useful car we ever owned, but it became intolerable to drive because of the stench from the dead chipmunk.

My son had the same thing happen to his car and he told us that after a year or two the stink would go away. I wasn't going to allow that vehicle to smell like that for a year or two. So I spent too many dollars at a car repair shop to have the entire air conditioning and heating system searched for the misguided chipmunk. After that, I set traps around the wheels of the vehicle and trapped twenty-seven chipmunks near that Expedition. I don't know what the attraction is.

The most exciting chipmunk moment occurred many years ago. I was going to take our Mini Astro-van to town. I turned the key to start the van and heard a snapping sound and then smoke started billowing out from under the hood. I pulled the hood latch immediately and jumped out of the van and saw a chipmunk scurry from the van. I lifted the hood and there in flames was a huge chipmunk nest. I grabbed a fire extinguisher and put the fire out before the entire engine compartment caught fire. I was shocked to learn the wiring that the chipmunk had chewed through, would cost me $300 to replace. So I fixed the harness myself by soldering the wires back together. I was able to replace most of the components with salvage yard parts.

I think the most effective solution to the chipmunks is to move the vehicles frequently and never park in the same spot.

Wilderness Adventure

Our friend Carrie told us a story of an experience she had when she first took a job as a wildlife biologist with IDFG. Carrie volunteered to help her male supervisor with a hike and a fishing trip for two male supporters of Fish and Game. The adventure included an overnight stay in the Snow Peak fire tower and a morning hike down the side of the mountain to fish for trout. The view from Snow Peak was well known for the spectacular panorama of Idaho's Mallard Larkin Mountain Range and watching mountain goats in the area.

The lengthy hike to Snow Peak and the climb up to the fire watch house was exhausting, but worth the trip for the view alone. The next step was to ready the inside of the watch house for a night of rest. Carrie decided she would be much more comfortable sleeping outside on the wooden perimeter walkway apart from the men.

As the men cleaned and readied the inside for a good night sleep they rousted out a mouse. The pesky rodent raced around the watch house avoiding the intruders, but was finally chased out the door and onto the walkway. With total darkness quickly approaching, Carrie was snug in her sleeping bag and ready for a good night of sleep. But, the displaced mouse scurried for cover and crawled into Carrie's sleeping bag. Now mice aren't that big, but the bag wasn't big enough for Carrie and the mouse, so quick as a flash Carrie was out of the sleeping bag. She shook the bag, the mouse fell out, ran down the walkway and out of sight. Carrie suspected that the little mouse just ran off the walkway and fell a hundred feet down.

At last Carrie got back in her sleeping bag and was ready for a night of rest. Just as she was falling asleep, she heard the clop, clop, clop, clop of something in the dark coming up the stairway to the deck around the fire tower. It was reminiscent of the giant pterodactyl in the movie Jurassic Park III coming out of the fog. What could it be? Suddenly there it was, just a few feet from her. It was another resident of the northern Rockies, a nanny mountain goat. In the moonlight Carrie could see the nanny getting too close for comfort. She yelled at it, "Go away, go away." Finally it backed down the steps. It returned again and again, each time just as she was about to fall asleep. Finally the goat gave up and Carrie fell asleep.

Unfortunately, when Carrie did wake up she had an aching nose. There on the tip of her nose were two teeth marks. The vengeful mouse had returned and bit her on the nose. When Carrie spotted the mouse, it ran off to a small hole in the fire tower.

Soon the men woke up from a restful sleep. They made breakfast and were ready to get down the mountain to trout fish. As exhausted as Carrie was from the goat and mouse adventure, she did her best to ensure that the guests enjoyed the day of fishing and made it through the lengthy hikes down one mountain, up another mountain and then out to the vehicle.

The Guard Owl

Over the years, owls were the most common raptor that Beth rehabbed or raised. The types included great horned, barred, pygmy, saw whet, screech and barn owls. In Iowa, one of the first was a great horned owl brought to us by a local farmer. It was a baby and it had been blown out of its nest during a storm. In some cases like that, if the parents can find the baby owl, called an owlet, they'll care for it. This time, the parents didn't find the owlet and it was soon in poor health. So when the farmer gave it to us it was near death. We named it Barney.

Barney took to our presence immediately and was a ravenous eater. We fed it mice, unprocessed chicken and beef and fish. Included in Barney's diet were vitamin supplements, especially calcium, to insure proper bone growth. That fact is often overlooked by people who have illegally taken wildlife home thinking they are doing good, when in fact, they end up causing serious developmental problems to the animal which often leads to death. Barney would wolf food down like there was no tomorrow. It grew rapidly and when it had its full complement of flight feathers, we let him loose in our garage to practice flying. After that we opened the garage door to allow Barney to fly in and out of our garage while still providing food. Our home was in the country where there were plenty of trees to fly back and forth too. Barney preferred to roost in the garage where he wouldn't be hassled by songbirds. Barney would test his prowess in the outdoors at night, but continued to spend days in the garage.

One sunny afternoon in late summer, Barney was on its favorite roost in the garage, a step ladder. Our two younger children played in the front yard in front of the open garage, while we were tending our nearby garden. Unseen by us, a large stray dog wandered into our yard through the side woods. When the dog saw the two youngsters, it growled as it slowly approached them. Before they could call for us, Barney came swooping out of the garage on a strafing pattern toward the dog. The surprised dog turned and ran down our driveway toward the neighborhood lane with Barney in pursuit. At the last moment the owl opened its talons, but the terrified dog was able to avoid getting a butt load of great horned owl talons. Barney maxed out its flight range and landed at the end of our graveled drive way.

We heard the kids call for us at the same time that we heard the scrambling of the dog's paws on the concrete pad in front of the garage. We sped to the house just in time to see the finish of the owl vs dog challenge. We also watched the dog as it ran down the neighborhood lane to the county road a half mile away. When we reached the kids, they were laughing about Barney the guard owl that chased the dog from our yard, perhaps saving one or both of them from being bitten. Barney was sitting on the driveway recovering from his mission to rid the yard of a stray dog. After recovering, Barney flew back to the ladder in the garage, his mission accomplished.

We continued to feed Barney for a few more days, but realized that the owl was getting ready for its new life. Barney roosted in a tall eastern red cedar for a few days and then moved to even taller trees nearby. Two days later Barney the guard owl was off on his own.

Eerie Orca Encounter

Quite some time ago I took a boat ride with a friend from Kodiak Harbor to Uganik Island, Alaska to hunt Sitka black-tail deer. As we motored through Whale Pass and off Whale Island, a pod of orca were a few hundred yards from our starboard bow. We watched the amazing animals for a few minutes and my friend told me an interesting story that he described as eerie.

He and another friend were on a similar journey through the same waters when a pod of orca came alongside them. The orcas came exceptionally close and when they were too close for comfort for this nineteen foot skiff (a kind of boat), the boat owner slowed to a stop. He was afraid that the orcas may make an unexpected move or that he would hit an orca with his boat or prop, possibly injuring an orca or damaging his skiff. The orcas disappeared for a few moments until two gradually rose to the surface and glided a short distance to the side of his boat. The orcas were so close he could have touched one of them with his hand.

The boat driver looked intently at the closest one and it looked him in the eye. They were eye to eye and he said the intensity of the orcas glare was uncanny. He said he had this eerie feeling that although he could not communicate directly with the animal it had a level of intelligence that man could never comprehend. Eventually the orca sunk out of sight and was not seen again. My friend said he had never heard of anyone that had a similar experience with orcas in the wild.

Do You Believe?

One's spiritual belief is their own. I have my own spiritual belief that I was helped by the Holy Spirit to find a dog. Our youngest daughter at age seven found a mixed breed dog that she named Pam. Pam was a small dog that looked like it was a poodle schnauzer mix. It had a chubby body with short legs and was as lovable as they come. The vet guessed that the little dog was about 1 year old when found. Pam and our daughter were always together until our daughter went away to college. At that time, Pam stayed with us and saw our daughter when she came home from college occasionally.

When Pam was fourteen years old, the old dog had a stroke. She would walk in circles or walk into a corner and not be able to find her way out. She had trouble eating and we hand fed her with soft foods. According to a veterinarian there was no hope for recovery. Our daughter came home from college for Christmas and semester break and spent a lot of time taking care of her old friend, but there was little improvement.

January came quickly and Pam was not better. When our two dogs needed to go outside, someone in the family had to be with Pam and guide her back into the house. One evening, I took the dogs out and thought I'd get some firewood too. It was a cold January evening with about two feet of snow on the ground. I shoveled out a small circle from the snow and put Pam in the circle to do her business. I was sure that she would stay there since it was surrounded by a two foot wall of snow. I took my eye off of her for a second to get the firewood and she was gone into the dark. Our daughter was at work and would be home around midnight. How could we tell her that we lost her sick old dog.

Beth and I searched for Pam for hours before we went back in the house. I was upset that I didn't pay better attention to her and believed it was my fault she was gone. I vowed I'd go back out and not return until I found her. I said a prayer and asked God for guidance. Our house is on top of a bench that drops off steeply to an area that has a stream in the spring. The snow was crusty, so it was possible for the small dog to walk on top of the crust and leave no tracks. With a flashlight in hand I walked directly down the bench from where I last saw her. Once on the bottom I searched for her in the vicinity of the seasonal stream. It didn't take long for me to find Pam's footprints, they were clear as day on the crusty snow. I followed the tracks a short distance and there she was, under a tree, in a spot void of snow in the dry stream bed. I found her less than 10 minutes from when I started my second search. I put her cold body inside my jacket and walked back up the hill to home.

The next day I showed Beth where I found Pam, but while my footprints were quite visible, the little dog's tracks could not be seen anywhere, not even near the tree where she had been lying. We looked and looked, but saw nothing that was close to a dog footprint. They were so apparent the night before and now they were gone. It hadn't snowed nor had the wind-blown to cover them. There is no explanation for how the tracks disappeared. Were they ever there? Call it what you will, but I will always believe the Holy Spirit guided me to that little dog.

After that night, Pam started to get better and she recovered completely to eat, go in and out of the house as before and even play like a pup again. She lived another 3 years until the age of seventeen.

Bigfoot

The legend of Bigfoot, whether you believe in it or not, is always an interesting topic of discussion. Some cryptozoologists believe in its existence while others claim it's either a folklore creature or a hoax. Television documentaries and books have been dedicated to this creature and I know several Idaho Fish and Game Conservation Officers who have kept records of Bigfoot reports.

When my son Jon first started hunting in north Idaho we'd always start the deer season hunting mule deer in the high country. One winter morning, we were in the Selkirk Mountains about a half a mile from the Canada border. We were on a logging trail working our way through eight inches of snow. Our pace was slow as we searched for mule deer when Jon stopped abruptly and said, "Dad look, Bigfoot tracks." There in front of us were perfect impressions of human like foot prints about 16 inches long with a stride of about two and a half feet. We followed the tracks downhill, but when the tracks passed through brush it was difficult to trail further. We then traced them backward and uphill, but the result was the same. The best, almost perfect tracks were in the snow on the trail. One unique feature of these tracks, besides the length, was it only had four distinguishable toes and no claws.

At that same time, I had a Canadian colleague whose father-in-law was considered a Bigfoot expert. I sent a description of this event to this gentleman and he responded that the most likely explanation was a grizzly bear that walked in its own tracks (the front foot imprint followed by the imprint of the rear foot) and Bigfoot would have had a much longer stride. Even with snow on the ground it isn't unusual for bears to come out of their den for a short time only to return to it. I still wonder, if it was a grizzly, why weren't there any claw marks?

On another occasion we were showing friends some scenic sites in north Idaho. One site was an old growth forest near Pritchard, Idaho. It was early spring and some places still had snow on the ground. One large spot of snow had an abundance of wildlife tracks. I was pointing out the differences in deer, elk and moose tracks when we saw human-like foot prints. They were about eight to ten inches in length. I cannot believe they were from a bear because once again there were no claws. Could they have been a hoax?

There was one other eerie unexplainable event that I experienced. On a warm summer evening, I decided I would hop in our hot tub to relax before bedtime. By habit I always searched our yard with a flashlight for wildlife and occasionally I'd see something. On this occasion, July 2014, I saw a pair of green eyes near the trees at the furthest extent of our yard. This was downright spooky, because the eyes were behind a deer exclosure Beth built to protect her blue berries from deer. The fence of the exclosure is about five and a half feet high and the eyes were an easy two feet higher. I continued to follow the pair of eyes until they disappeared into a valley below our house.

Our friend Eliisa told us about her Bigfoot sighting. At the time she and her husband lived near Priest Lake. She was traveling home one night when suddenly a human-like creature walked out of the woods into her head lights. It continued onto the road directly in front of her. She slowed and the upright creature walked across the road, unafraid of the car lights. She described it as tall, covered with dark hair, hominid looking and walked bipedal similar to a human.

I understand that people who haven't had these experiences may think it comical to talk of such an animal. Perhaps someday we'll know the truth.

When Terror Overwhelms Your Senses

I have witnessed two circumstances when friends were so terrified that their fear took over their common sense. On one occasion I was fishing with friends in a 14 foot boat on a backwater of the Wisconsin River. Fishing was very slow and it was late afternoon when I noticed a large northern water snake swimming toward us. When it was less than ten feet from the boat I casually said, "Look, a water snake."

After hearing "snake" one friend said with fear in his voice, "A snake." He looked at the snake and started to step over the other side of the boat to enter the water. I grabbed him and pulled him back into the boat. He was shaking and was absolutely terrified of the snake. He later told me snakes were his biggest fear in life, a phobia. I didn't understand the behavior of leaving the safety of the boat to enter the water the snake was in thinking he was going to escape from it until I did some research. A phobic fear will overwhelm a person's rational thought process. I also talked to individuals that have clinical phobias and I understand much better. The phobic reaction of the individuals is completely irrational and they may do something totally unexpected to save themselves. The fear of snakes is called ophidiophobia or ophiophobia It is sometimes called herpetophobia, fear of reptiles or amphibians.

The phobia – an irrational or overwhelming fear – is distinct from a general dislike of snakes and from reasonable fear of venomous snake bites or of the danger posed by large constrictors like boas and pythons. An ophidiophobe not only fears snakes when in live contact but also dreads to think about them or even see them in video or still pictures.

On the second occasion I was fishing with friends near the Indian River off the coast of Delaware. We were about ten miles off shore and we had a great day of fishing. We were slowly motoring our way in when I saw two seven foot bull sharks at 30 yard starboard of the boat. I said, "Look, a pair of bull sharks."

The boat owner's thirty-year old son, a Navy veteran, yelled, "Sharks." After seeing the sharks he ran from the starboard side of the boat to the port side where I was and proceeded to lift a leg over the gunwale to enter the water thinking he was going to avoid the sharks. Again, I grabbed him and pulled him down onto the deck.

The phobic fear of sharks is called Galeophobia. I read individuals that have this fear continue to experience persistently and irrationally thought and behavior processes. Thus, this explains the action of climbing out of the boat to avoid the shark but entering the water the sharks were in.

Deep Water Monster?

Lake Pend Oreille is one of the most beautiful and largest lakes in North America. The lake is also one of the most mysterious in North America and is about 1200 feet deep. Geologists still argue as to how this 94,000 acre body of water was created. The U.S. Navy established a research station on the lake many years ago to test submarine detection systems and more.

Many years ago my crew and I were using a large 10 x 10 foot trawl net and towing it behind a large boat in open water at the south end of Lake Pend Oreille. We were trawling to sample young kokanee salmon and the net was set at about 60 feet in depth in about 500 feet of water. We used a graph recorder as a tool to mark submerged inanimate objects and fish. The lake is a world class Kamloops rainbow trout fishery, so from time to time we would mark one of the 20 to 30 inch trout, as well as the smaller kokanee salmon. As we passed over the sampling location with the net deployed I noticed an object on our graph recorder. The object gave the same signature as a fish, an inverted V shape. I called the crew to the recorder and we were all astonished as to the huge size of the signature. It suggested the object was likely fish shaped and we estimated 15 to 20 feet in length. When I showed the recording to research scientists at the Navy's research station they had no explanation and told me it was not one of their drone submarines. You can use your imagination on that story.

The Bug

One warm morning when I was an undergraduate at Iowa State University, a friend and I decided we would take a different route than usual to our first class of the day. We walked the main east- west route through town. We were having the typical guy discussion about weekend dates when he interrupted our conversation. He saw a giant water bug on the edge of the curb and before I could say a word he had the insect in his hand. Just as I said it's a giant predacious water bug, the insect sunk it's proboscis into the palm of his hand. My friend let out a wale that would terrify Dracula. He shook his hand and the large bug fell off. It was huge, almost two inches long and to this day I have never seen one larger.

My college buddy opened the palm of his hand and there was a hole about an eighth of an inch in diameter and bleeding profusely. I went to class and he went to the infirmary where he was treated. Within a short time my friend's hand swelled to an immense size and he was in severe pain. It was nearly two weeks before his hand recovered and he was told he was lucky that a serious infection had not started.

The giant predacious water bug is an aquatic insect with wings making them mobile. In nature, they will attack fish, crayfish or tadpoles by grasping ahold of their prey with their legs and then piercing the quarry with its proboscis and proceed to suck the fluid out of the victim.

An Aggressive Bobcat

My stepfather grew up in the small town of Broadalbin in up-state New York. He enjoyed hunting and fishing and time in the woods in New York and later in Wisconsin. He had many stories - some of which were believable.

A story that remained in my memory was an encounter my stepfather's brother and a companion had with a bold bobcat. The pair was hiking in the dark to their hunting camp deep in the woods of the Adirondack Mountains. They had rifles and flashlights in hand while the rest of their gear was in back packs. As they followed the trail to their camp they heard something walking in the dry leaves, apparently following them. They'd stop and the animal tracking them would stop. Each hunter drew a hand weapon from their pack. The lead hunter had a knife while the trailing hunter had a hand axe.

As they continued on their way a huge bobcat dropped out of a tree onto the lead man without warning. The weight and momentum of the cat caused the hunter to fall forward. With a flashlight in his left hand and the axe in his right, the trailing hunter took a swipe at the attacking cat and killed it with his second strike. The lead hunter was not injured. For whatever reason, from time to time this smaller of the North American cats can become emboldened and attack humans. Bobcats should never be considered docile animals.

My stepfather told me one other story in which a young girl from a nearby town was killed by a bobcat. The incident he said happened at night and the cat was unprovoked. When I was working for IDFG we'd hear reports from hunters who claimed a mountain lion had followed them or they had killed a lion that they thought would attack them. When we investigated these stories, the lions were often young animals that may not have ever seen a human before. Most likely the animal was trying to determine if the person was a food item. That is one good reason it is best to walk away, not run, from a predator. It's believed running only stimulates the pursuit response in the predator. After my son's encounter with the wolves and other stories I've heard, I always carry, not in a back pack, an easily accessible hand gun.

Elliott the Elk

The smell of alfalfa must permeate the woods like that of a heavy dose of a woman's perfume in a bar. Beth feeds the livestock twice a day, but in winter deer can be seen at the edge of the woods waiting for her to toss the hay to our animals. Not only are deer attracted to the scent of alfalfa, but nearby elk are too. Our barnyard animals tolerated deer munching with them for years, but never had the much larger elk come in their corral before.

One hard winter, a spike elk came. He appeared one morning and hung around the edge of the corral eating bits of hay. We did not think too much about it because we did not think the spike elk would come back after the day was over. The next day when Beth fed her llama and two dwarf goats, the elk showed up again. He started to be a regular visitor in the corral with several deer. We decided to call the daily guest Elliott the Elk. After a week or more, Elliott started to get bolder and move closer to the large pile of alfalfa in front of Lolly, the llama. Now Lolly was always able to keep the deer away from her food as she was a little larger than they were, but now she was approached by a much larger creature. Elliott edged closer to her food, she raised her head and gave him the stare. Usually that worked on the smaller animals, but not this time. Elliott wanted that pile of alfalfa. The young elk came close to the llama. Beth watched from the kitchen window and saw Lolly spit a large gob of llama juice right into the elk's face.

Elliott had never experienced that before and he turned around and ran toward the far corner of the corral. Beth thought he would jump over the fence and return to the safety of the woods. Elliott stopped at the fence and stared at the woods, then he turned his head and stared at the llama standing guard by her alfalfa. The elk then looked at the woods for a while and then turned his head to look at the food. He did that for a full 20 minutes, it was if he was debating the merits of eating or escaping into the woods. Finally, the elk turned completely around and walked slowly back toward the alfalfa. Lolly was still standing over it. Elliott now knew what he was up against. The elk put his head down and moved his large body toward the llama so whatever she would spit at him would miss his face. A confused llama backed closer to the barn, leaving the rest of the alfalfa by the elk.

Elliott stayed in our yard for a month and would appear in the mornings and afternoons during feeding time. While Beth brought hay out for the critters, the lone elk waited at the edge of the woods trying to blend in with the brush and tree branches, but Beth saw him and called out, "Hello Elliott". Before Beth even left the barn area and walked toward the house, Elliott and half a dozen deer already jumped the fence and mingled in the corral with the llama and the two goats. Lolly did not challenge Elliott anymore and there seemed to be a truce. One day a single cow elk appeared in the yard and two days later Elliott disappeared and did not return. I guess there were more important things to do then.

Picture 9. Elliot at the receiving end of a giant gob of llama juice.

Picture 10. Elliot the elk, three whitetail deer, goats Sugar and Spice and Lolly Llama share a meal of alfalfa.

DUMB STUFF

,

Denali Moose Rampage

Beth and I took a vacation to Alaska and one of our destinations was Denali National Park. Wildlife was abundant including brown bear, Dall sheep and moose. At that time the only means of transportation in Denali National Park, for the public, was by a park bus system. So our movement from point to point was governed by the bus schedule. While waiting for a bus, I had conversation with a Park Ranger who explained what an issue they had with tourists and wildlife. The tourists had no respect for the animals and would get too close. "Like that guy," said the Ranger.

I looked across the road and there was a man approaching several cow moose with calves. Just as the ranger started toward the problem tourist, the cows and calves ran at the man. He turned tail and ran with the cows breathing down his neck. He reached a huge downed fir tree and dove under it shielding himself from the rampaging cows. When the cows finally gave up on the idea of stomping on the man, he emerged very proud of himself. He was proud that is until the ranger chewed him out. It turns out that this trouble maker was a park ranger at the Great Smokey Mountains National Park and he became very apologetic.

Old People Can Sprint

On the very same trip to Denali, as the previous moose story, Beth and I witnessed an older couple in their 70s run at warp speed. Beth and I were sitting in a park bus waiting for it to move on when we watched an older couple leave their van, with the doors open, and walk out to a magnificent bull moose. It was in the rut tearing up vegetation and shredding bushes and small trees with its huge palmated antlers. I could see the woman had a Brownie Instamatic camera, you know the kind you have to get within three feet of a person to fill the frame. The woman kept getting closer and closer while the bull paid no attention to them. Suddenly the bull turned and charged them. They both spun 180 degrees and high-tailed it to their van. I thought there was total certainty the bull would catch them and tear them to shreds. But to my surprise the couple hit warp speed and out distanced the bull. Upon reaching the van the woman literally jumped through the air into the open passenger side and with one clean sweep closed the door behind her. The bull continued and when it appeared he was going to hit the van he stopped inches from it. He turned in a rage with his eyes glazed over and tore up the turf and destroyed a large bush next to the van. Never in my life did I ever see two old people run faster than the late Bob Hayes.

A Cougar Lives in my Yard

Mountain lions are common in north Idaho, but secretive. In 28 years of living in north Idaho I've only seen two mountain lions. Our Regional Fish and Game Office in Coeur d'Alene takes many wildlife calls from the public. Some calls are complaints, other calls are just questions and yet other calls are reports of dead or injured wildlife for employees to retrieve.

On this particular morning our office manager took a call from a woman that lived near a secluded village on the east shore of Lake Pend Oreille. The caller complained of a mountain lion that had been regularly prowling around her property from the nearby National Forest land. The caller wanted the agency to trap the cougar and take it far away from her location. The Fish and Game employee wanted to get as much information about the situation as possible. "Cougars do not normally stay near humans," said our manager. "There has to be a reason why the cougar prowls around your home."

With further questioning, the caller explained that the cougar was hunting the raccoons that frequented the porch of the caller's home. IDFG should do something about it. Again our manager quizzed her further. How had she witnessed so many raccoons being eaten by the lion? The irate caller explained, "I watched from the kitchen window." The intrigued employee continued, "Why are the raccoons coming to your porch?" The woman finally confessed that she had been feeding the raccoons oatmeal cookies that she baked every day. Then the lion showed up. When told that she needed to stop feeding the raccoons oatmeal cookies so that all of the animals would search for natural food, she still insisted the lion should be relocated. She was told that even if this lion was moved away, another lion would just start the same pattern. Nature abhors a vacuum.

Bobcats May be Cute But...

A friend told me the following story. A few years back a rural northeast Washington man noticed a bobcat frequenting his backyard. It was not known why the cat hung around. The bobcat was beautiful and the man wanted to befriend it – and tame it. He thought, "What a gorgeous pet it would make." So the man decided to coax the wild cat into his house; he would feed it some meat in a bowl and gradually move the bowl closer to the house and eventually inside his home.

The man initiated his plan. He placed of few chunks of meat in a bowl near the location he most often saw the bobcat. The cat was slow to take the meat at first, but it was an easy meal. On the second day he moved the bowl closer to his home. Gradually the bobcat became habituated to finding his bowl of meat. Then came the day to catch the wild bobcat; the foolish man left his door open and placed the bowl inside the house. The bobcat cautiously stepped into the house and walked to the bowl of meat. It looked around and seeing no threats began to feast once more on the free meal. Just as the bobcat was finishing up the man closed the door. Suddenly there was no way out. "My plan worked," thought the man, "and now I can further show the bobcat I am truly its friend and master. I'll be the talk of the neighborhood." He was right on one count-he was the talk of the neighborhood. Paramedics were soon called and the wanna-be animal trainer was rushed to the hospital. He had received numerous lacerations while the bobcat was unscathed. One lesson here is wild animals are called W-I-L-D animals for a reason. They should be left alone and viewed at a safe distance.

Where Was the Babysitter

Years ago when our first two kids were five and two years of age, we hired a babysitter that had been recommended. I'll call her Dina. Vaughn and the kids brought her to our house where I showed her around, gave her appropriate phone numbers and left the two kids in her care. Upon arriving home that night I asked Dina if the kids behaved and how things went. She replied that the kids spilled something in the kitchen, but she cleaned it up. Dina seemed quite nervous and in a hurry to get home, so Vaughn and our daughter drove her home. I went upstairs to check on our sleeping two year old son. When Vaughn and our daughter returned, they came directly upstairs.

The next morning, I went downstairs to start breakfast. As soon as I stepped into the kitchen my shoes stuck to the vinyl. I made my way toward the sink - each step was into stickier goo than the last one. When I reached the sink, I noticed the large bottle of dish detergent (which was full yesterday) was now nearly empty.

I had a good idea of what was spread all over the kitchen floor. As I tried to wipe up it up, the soap would turn into more foam and bubbles. Finally after 4 hours of wiping and rinsing, I was able to clean most of it up.

When the kids awoke, I heard the rest of the story. The previous evening, Dina, the baby sitter sat in the living room watching TV and doing homework.

Our two industrious youngsters decided to do some cleaning, starting with bathing the pet guinea pig. What would they use to wash the guinea pig? No problem, there's a full bottle of dish detergent. The kids pushed the kitchen chairs to the sink, took the guinea pig to the sink and poured on the soap. Somehow, soap slopped onto the floor.

The two kids thought it would be a nice surprise for mom if they cleaned the floor also. More dish detergent went onto the floor and spread all over the kitchen space.

Where was the babysitter?

"What are you two doing out there?" Dina yelled from the other room.

"We're just cleaning the guinea pig," they answered. Dina went back to her homework. The kids quickly put the guinea pig back in her cage and left the kitchen. When Dina later came to the kitchen to get the kids some orange juice, I think she discovered why they had been so quiet for such a long time.

When I heard that the guinea pig had been involved, I quickly went to her cage. To my horror, I saw that the poor pig was hunched up in a horseshoe shape. Her fur was stiff from dried dish detergent - it had not been rinsed out. I grabbed the pathetic animal and rushed to the sink and started to wet the fur with water. The soap bubbled up over and over and as I rinsed the pig, it squealed from pain. Finally she was clear of soap. I dried her in a towel – all the while wondering if she would live. Two weeks later the guinea pig's fur peeled off as if it was a prepared animal pelt. The guinea pig looked like a skinned rat. "The end is near for her," I thought. But no, not only did she survive, but in the next couple of months she grew a full body of fur. Post script – We never hired Dina again.

The Spotted Armenian Hodag

When I was an undergraduate at Iowa State University most of my friends knew I was interested in reptiles and amphibians. A friend brought me a small tiger salamander he had snatched off a county road. I made a terrarium for my new pet and kept it in my dorm room. I fed it worms, hamburger and occasionally locusts, moths and grasshoppers. For lack of a better name my roommate Phil dubbed it the Spotted Armenian Hodag (not to be confused with the legendary Hodag of Rhinelander, Wisconsin). Phil told the other dormies to stay away from the "Hodag" because its bite was fatal. From time to time a freshman would stick his finger in front of the animal's nose and since the salamander couldn't tell a fat worm from a fat finger with lightning speed it would bite the fat finger. Phil would laugh and tell the kid that he would now die within the hour. I'd ask the kid if he would give me his favorite sweater since he'd no longer need it.

During the summer I took the salamander with me wherever my temporary job with Wisconsin Department of Natural Resources would take me. All along the Hodag was growing. I had it until the fall of 1969 when I was drafted into the Army. I gave the salamander to my younger brother David and he cared for it more than a year. By the spring of 1971, the amphibian was enormous stretching almost 13 inches in length. At that time our mother demanded that David release it.

Chipmunk Bite

One afternoon Pete, our family cat, caught a chipmunk in the yard. Pete played with the chipmunk for a while and when my mother found Pete with the chipmunk, the little rodent was near death – or so she thought. My mother took the exhausted chipmunk from the cat and held it in her hand. She gently rotated the chipmunk holding its head up. She stroked its head and said, "Poor, poor chipmunk, it's almost dead." Just then it bit her thumb. Blood was pouring from her thumb like it was cut with a knife. My mother immediately dropped the chipmunk and it hit the floor running-- with the cat in hot pursuit. The chipmunk ran out the open door and into a hole. My mother's thumb required several stitches. After that incident my mother and stepfather showed chipmunks no mercy.

Loose Cannon

When we lived in Iowa Beth worked for a county conservation department as the wildlife educator. On the weekends she did double duty as a county park fee collector on weekends. From time to time I'd substitute for her and I also sold fire wood for the county for campers. I called it my "village idiot job." One Friday evening, I worked at the park. I knew that the county had just hired a former Deputy Sheriff for weekend security. He was a big burly guy that earned the nickname, Cannon.

I was right on time for collecting camping fees and selling fire wood to the weekend campers at the park. It was a very nice county park with play areas for kids, room for a ball field, and a trout stream for fishing. For some reason, this weekend had exceptionally low attendance. I had had two of our three children with me as I drove in. I immediately saw the security man in a county pickup truck and thought I would introduce myself. After exchanging introductions Cannon told me he was searching for a stray dog that was reported by campers as dogs were not allowed to run in the parks. As we talked he suddenly shouted, "There he is," and spun off in pursuit of the hapless dog. I followed close behind to see how he was going to handle the situation.

The dog was sniffing near a garbage can. Cannon parked near a rest room on the park road. Cannon exited his truck and drew his .38 Colt. I jumped out of my truck and started to question the use of a gun with campers around. The dog rolled over to its back and looked like a giant roach. It was shaking like a leaf in that well known submissive position. I started to tell Cannon not to shoot, just grab the dog, when a loud B-A-N-G sounded. He had shot at the dog point blank range and only clipped its ear. The terrified dog jumped up and ran toward the east where the park road turns into a cul-de-sac. The dog ran around the cul-de-sac and back the way it came from straight to Cannon. Cannon gave every excuse in the book, why he missed the dog. He was determined to snuff the life out of the wounded dog with a round from his .38. The dog suddenly realized he was back with Cannon. The dog immediately ran under a campers parked car, shaking like a leaf by the gas tank. I said, "Don't shoot the dog it's too dangerous."

"I'm getting this dog! Everyone stand back," he ordered. I grabbed my two children and hustled them into our truck. I turned and I heard another B-A-N-G. In a microsecond, the dog howled as it came out from under the car but apparently untouched by Cannon's .38 slug. The dog ran straight for the stream bank. It didn't know there was a 16 foot cliff at the edge where it was headed. In a flash, the dog disappeared as it sailed over the cliff. I ran to the cliff with Cannon close behind – loaded gun and all. The dog was not seen for the rest of the day.

That next morning, the wounded dog showed up at a camp site. It was moaning and whining from fear and pain. It drew considerable sympathy and was taken to a local veterinarian. The vet tended to the dog and held it for the rest of the weekend. Monday morning, the vet called the director of the park and asked him to pick up his dog and pay the vet bills. The director was furious. He asked me what had happened. I explained all the foolishness and dangerous shooting, despite my warning Cannon. The following week, Cannon was fired after numerous campers complained that he was too overbearing. As for the dog, he ended up with the county animal control people and his destiny was - your guess is as good as mine.

Dumb Gets Dumber

Everyone hears stories of people getting killed by wild animals in our State and National parks. I've seen fathers try to place their three or four year old toddlers on the back of buffalo for a photo. I once saw a man from Germany try to pet a moose in Yellowstone National Park while his wife took a picture. The man was lucky the annoyed moose ran off and didn't attack him.

My stepfather, Bill, was not known to be a good decision maker. He was the only one I ever knew that actually sawed off a branch of a tree while he was balancing on the branch. I had warned him the branch would give way, but he ignored me. He cut the branch, fell with the running chain saw buzzing and just missed by inches whacking his nose off. For whatever reason, he never heeded a word I ever said.

Now comes one of my favorite stories on Bill. Northern Wisconsin is home to thousands of black bears. In the old days it was evening entertainment for tourists to go to the county dump and watch bears feed on piles of garbage. We did the same, but except for my stepfather--he took it further. He was determined he was going to show off (which always back fired) and ride one of the burley bruins. As everyone waited at the edge of the garbage dump in the safety of cars the bears filed out of the woods and proceeded to sort through the trash looking for a morsel; perhaps a piece of stale pizza or a spoiled hoagie.

One hungry bear gradually worked his way in front of our car and Bill decided it was show time. He got out of the car and walked up to the food focused black bear. Feeling brave or stupid, Bill attempted to straddle the animal just as the brute moved. Bill missed the target and rolled to the ground, fortunately the bear cared less. Bill got up to try again and looked at us as if to say, "See me, I'm cool." During this drama my mother was screaming her head off, telling him to get back in the car. On his second try Bill succeeded getting on the bear's back. The bear didn't like the added weight and wheeled around to slam Bill, but he fell off the opposite side.

When reality set in, Bill picked himself up and ran to the car with the bear giving chase. It was the first time in 15 years that I ever saw Bill run. Bill opened his driver side door and slammed it shut in the bears face.

The angry bear found a foam ball on the tip of the car's radio antenna and snapped the antenna off the car. When we told him how dumb his actions were he bragged about his foot speed. But the angry bear had the last laugh, so to speak, he found the foam ball and ate it and Bill had to buy a new radio antenna.

One Tough Buck

One of the most ridiculous stories I ever heard from an IDFG conservation officer was of a very ignorant hunter. The officer had an ASA set up off a road that typically had a lot of illegal road hunting (an ASA is an animated simulated animal that has robotic parts). He sat well concealed but in a safe location. A truck with a hunter drove by and then slowed. The hunter got out of the truck and instead of stepping off the road way proceeded to raise his rifle and make an illegal shot at the buck ASA. The ASA didn't move and thinking he had missed the hunter now in clear violation and video recorded proceeded to shoot again and again. No, despite the officer telling him not to shoot anymore, he continued shooting emptying his rifle. The violator proceeded to reload as the officer again told him to stop shooting. Having no clue that he was in violation he looked at the officer and said can you believe I missed that buck five times and it's still just standing out there. The officer responded yes and that it was not a live animal and wrote the violator a ticket for shooting from a roadway.

Some Pranks Aren't Funny

After the bear incident (Teddy, the Troublesome Brown Bear), Pete and I were a little more cautious when it came to watching bears. I devised a box mechanism for my camera so I could take pictures of bears without having to be there; a similar principal as modern trail cameras. The system worked for my 35 mm Yoshika and I was able to take a few night pictures of brown bears. Pete liked the system and built one for his Kodak Instamatic.

My preferred areas for setting the camera box were a mile or more from our cabin. Pete decided he would try his camera on Spring Creek, which was only 50 yards from the cabin.

Pete was excited to try his camera box and set it up during the day. He planned to check it at night. Evening came and Pete went to retrieve his camera and reset it if it was tripped. Bears were very busy that time of year day or night, catching salmon with a lot of chasing other bears. I saw Pete leave the cabin without a rifle and I had an idea for a prank. The trail he used was a typical bear trail that was like a dry canal worn down from the thousands of years of bear use. I thought I would be funny and wait in the dark along the trail and then as he passed by leap out and grab his leg. It worked. Pete walked by unsuspecting that I could be that evil. I jumped out, grabbed his leg and shook it. He responded verbally with a shriek. I have to admit it may have been funny to me at the time, but it was a bad idea. When Pete realized it was me he was furious. In hind sight I would have been very upset too.

A few weeks later Pete got his revenge. We often watched bears from the roof of our cabin as they fished the Karluk River or traveled through the surrounding alders. Our privy was within the alders 30 yards behind the cabin. One late afternoon I was walking the trail to the privy while Pete was on the cabin roof watching bears. As I walked the trail Pete yelled, "Vaughn, stop. You're walking toward a bear and he sees you." I froze in my tracks. Because the trail was enclosed within the wall of alders I couldn't see any bears. Then Pete said, "Back up slowly." I responded and backed up all along looking for the bear. "Stop," he yelled. "There's a second bear closing in from your left in back of you. Go ahead walk slowly back." I resumed my goal to reach the cabin's safety. Then he yelled, "There's a third bear and they're all coming for you. Run Vaughn run." I turned and ran as fast as I could down the trail to the cabin. I looked up and saw Pete laughing so hard that he almost rolled off the roof. I guess we were even on pranks.

Foolish Homeowners

We're telling you a few sad stories only because we want to reach people to help them understand how difficult humans have made it for wildlife. People have expanded into the habitats of wildlife and have become selfish with no respect to the needs of God's beautiful creatures. Wildlife habitat continues to diminish with homes and buildings being built in critical areas of wildlife nesting, food, rearing and winter range so important to the existence of wildlife.

It's not uncommon for whitetail deer to be injured in or near neighborhoods. An injured animal is a pitiful sight that even an avid hunter does not like to see. Deer that live near humans have other hazards besides traffic.

Wire fences may be dangerous to deer as they attempt to jump over, they sometimes get their hind legs caught between wire strands and get trapped. If they aren't released soon enough, the trapped animals struggle and may die. A second type of fence that poses a problem is a fence with vertical bars of wrought iron or pipe. Young deer see the vertical opening, try to escape between the bars, and although their heads may fit between the rails, their shoulders or hind quarters won't and they get tightly wedged leading to severe injury and death. If property owners need to have fencing, consider the type, the height and the spacing between rails of the fencing and make sure the fence does not turn into a wildlife death trap.

Some people disdain seeing wildlife in their yards and carry out extreme measures to get rid of the problem. A sad situation occurred in an urban area when an individual decided to reduce the neighborhood deer population by shooting them at night and leaving them to die. Another property owner decided to scare off a doe in his yard by shooting at her with what he called a BB gun. He shot at her, hit her back and paralyzed her. The gun he used turned out to be a high powered air rifle. The man was regretful, but it was too late, the doe had to be put out of its misery.

The Japanese Yew Plant is Toxic for Wildlife

Every winter moose are killed by vehicles and trains. It is particularly common when we have a heavy snow fall. The roadways and railways are usually cleared for traffic, but that also makes it easier for wildlife movement too. The other problem that comes with winter's deep snow is wildlife, including moose, will venture closer to homes, rural and urban.

One winter evening, we were called by a neighbor who reported that a cow moose had been shot. It was lying on the ground near a home. We drove to the site of the animal and were told the story of the moose. The moose had been sick because it ate some Japanese Yew. Japanese Yew is a toxic ornamental plant often planted around houses by landscapers and home owners. When an animal or person eats this plant, the toxin causes the nervous and digestive systems to fail and death ensues. This moose was thrashing around on the ground when a person shot the sick animal. The shooter explained the moose was suffering and continuously moaned as it writhed in agony. The description was very emotional for the shooter who said he agonized seeing the dying moose. The IDFG Officer did not cite the compassionate person, but warned him not to do it again, just call IDFG instead. This wasn't the only toxic plant case. Every winter, moose, deer, pronghorn and many other animals die from eating the toxic Yew. The tragedy is not only that there are Japanese Yew in many landscaped yards, but many landscapers and home owners are unaware of the toxicity of this ornamental plant. Thus, more wildlife will die from eating Japanese Yew or other toxic plants, unless an education program or legislation takes place to prevent the further planting of this toxic plant. The dumb thing is that even some companies that know that that yew is a dangerous plant still sell the plant in plant nurseries and still promote the planting of it in landscaping projects.

Read the Game Crossing Sign

Several years ago I heard about a letter to a newspaper editor written by a woman with concern for wildlife safety. In the letter she criticized the highway department for placing game crossing signs at highway locations where there was heavy vehicle traffic. She had noticed that at those locations, there seemed to be more animal deaths. In her letter, she recommended that the signs be placed on highway sections that have light traffic use, therefore the animals would be directed to use those locations to cross the road and then cars and trucks would pose little danger. She reasoned that by placing the signs on stretches of our roadways where traffic is heavy only increased injury and death of wild animals. WHAT?

The previous individual was as well informed as the person in California that wrote – Hunters should stop hunting and killing wild game to eat. They should buy their meat at the grocery store where meat is made. Hmmm really!

A MATTER OF SURVIVAL

Death from Above

Lake Pend Oreille is known to have an abundance of bald eagles in early winter that feast on spawned out kokanee salmon. One sunny day, I was ice fishing with friends at the north end of the lake at a spot called Sunnyside. While fishing, I watched an injured coot in open water about 100 yards from us. It was exposed in the open water and was eventually spotted by an immature bald eagle. The eagle made a sweeping pass at the coot which quickly dove under the water.

This process went on and on for about 10 minutes before the eagle tired and flew a quarter mile to rest in a tall cottonwood tree. The coot rested near the ice where we were fishing and then without warning time was up. The eagle came back to finish its job. It dove at the doomed coot several more times before sinking its talons into the injured bird. The predator then flew to the cotton woods and had lunch. Nature is not like some city folks think; calm and serene. Rather it is a matter of survival everyday, whether from snow storms that make foraging energy consuming or a bobcat in pursuit of a snowshoe hair.

For a few years, after several mild winters, the population of valley quail around our acreage blossomed into a covey of over thirty birds. We fed them as well as turkeys and song birds with sunflower seeds. In the dead of winter, birds took advantage of our birdfeeders. As many birders know bird feeders also provide a benefit to raptors. On occasion, the birds at the bird feeder lose their instinctive concern for predators while competing for the free dinner. Like many other people, we enjoy the variety of birds we get at our feeders and one snowy morning was especially memorable.

A northern goshawk took note of the valley quail and made a pass over them nearly catching one. The covey burst for cover and flew to a nearby brush pile that we built for small game cover. The goshawk gave chase and landed near the brush pile. The raptor then walked in the snow as close as it could get to the brush pile, then balanced on its left foot while reaching into the brush pile with its right foot to snare a quail. The goshawk moved about the brush pile trying over and over to snag a quail with its new hunting technique. I watched the goshawk for close to an hour before it flew to a tree and waited. I don't know if it ever caught one of the little birds that day as I gave up watching before the raptor gave up waiting.

Leave My Chicks Alone

This story came from Dwain a retired IDFG Conservation Officer. Dwain was on patrol one morning on a Forest Service road when he noticed a covey of young ruffed grouse chicks in the middle of the well-traveled road. Dwain was concerned that a vehicle would come down the road and run over a chick or two. He got out of his truck and spread his arms to coax them off the road. Without warning a kamikaze ruffed grouse hen blasted him in the chest. The bird fell to the ground and threatened Dwain with another attack so he backed up. All he wanted to do was help her babies and all she wanted to do was protect them.

Serpent Battle

Some very peculiar outcomes can occur when snakes battle over a single food item and it can be chilling. Not many years ago, I witnessed a serpent battle. I have goldfish in my garden pond and I often see garter snakes hunting the goldfish. They are excellent hunters in the water and eat plenty of my goldfish each summer. In fact, I put several dozen feeder goldfish in the pond each year just to act as a buffer for my larger fish.

One afternoon I was slowly walking by the pond and I noticed some action at the edge. I moved closer and there were two garter snakes battling over one goldfish. The snakes were each attached to the fish. The larger snake was physically lifting and shaking the goldfish which caused the smaller snake to be smacked against the rocks lining the pond. I snapped several photos as the big snake continued to beat the smaller. It would have been difficult for the smaller snake to let go because a snake's teeth point in toward their throat. I left the scene to get a video camera and when I returned both snakes were gone, but left behind was a dead goldfish.

Boomerang Snakes

My friend Greg told me about the trouble he had with garter snakes in a garden pond. As he explained it, "We have a small fishpond behind our house that we try to keep stocked with goldfish for the pleasure of the grandkids.... as it turns out, the pond also provides pleasure to a healthy population of raccoons and garter snakes. We pretty much solved the raccoon problem by placing a couple of large cinder blocks (the kind with the big holes in the center) on the bottom of the pond. The raccoons still come by every now and then, but the fish were able to avoid becoming a meal by hiding inside the cinder blocks (despite the raccoons doing everything that they could to rearrange all of the pond decorations including the submersible pump).

The garter snakes proved to be a little more of a challenge, in that they were willing to lay in wait for hours on end until an unsuspecting goldfish swam within reach. Greg said, "If I would happen to walk by the pond while a snake was waiting for its fish, I could sometimes catch a snake (or sometimes as many as three at a time) by hand. Being kind of a snake lover, I wouldn't kill the snakes, but carry them off and turn them loose. My usual release site was at a small natural wet area about 150-200 yards away. My wife often laughed saying that I was just catching the same snakes over and over again while our goldfish population was slowly being consumed."

"In order to determine if the same snakes were indeed coming back after I released them, I started placing a small dot of fingernail polish on the top of their head (I knew that the dot would disappear when the snake shed its skin, but as it turned out it didn't have to last all that long). It only took a couple of days before I started seeing nail polish marked snakes back at our pond. I found it interesting that the snakes seemed to prefer a goldfish meal to foraging for more natural food at a nearby wetland".

My friend eventually took care of the snake problem by covering the pond with a wooden lattice and transporting any captured snakes by car several miles away.

Tuffy the Attack Grouse

Male Grouse are territorial birds especially in the spring before and during the breeding season. Every spring we have a few male ruffed grouse drumming someplace on our nine acres of woods.

One afternoon, a friend and I planned to go fishing and he was towing his boat behind his vehicle. Because we have a long private lane with a curve he parked below our house on the county road and began to walk up. He didn't get far before a male ruffed grouse came out of the woods and started chasing him. My friend stopped and turned and the grouse proceeded to peck at my friend's feet. I came down the road a few minutes later and the grouse was gone.

Several weeks went by and I didn't even think of the bird until one afternoon I was cutting firewood below the house when a male grouse came to me clucking like a chicken. I went back to the house and told Beth and we brought him some sunflower seeds. We named the bird Tuffy and he readily took to our feeding him. Every time I cut firewood Tuffy would be there for his handout of sunflower seeds.

Soon winter came and it was time to plow snow from our driveway with my four-wheeler. That first snow fall was about four inches. I didn't get far down the hill when I got hit in the head. I was hit so hard that the blow knocked off my ball cap. At first I thought it was a snow ball. I looked around, saw no one and proceeded to plow snow again. I drove about 20 feet and was whacked in the head again. That was it, I decided I would get to the bottom of this, but when I scanned the area no one was around. I started to get on the four-wheeler and there was Tuffy standing in the snow, but a bit fluffed up. I greeted him and proceeded to plow snow again.

Over the next two years, Tuffy thumped me on the back of the head or on my back 13 more times. Beth and I took several videos of Tuffy's actions protesting the snow plow. However, Tuffy probably thumped the wrong beast by his third year because we never saw him again. We regularly see ruffed grouse and we assume they are Tuffy's offspring.

Battle for the Karluk Cabin

My six months in Alaska working with another biologist were full of adventure everyday with brown bears around every corner, huge red fox in the area and fascinating wildlife watching. Included in the wildlife watching was the opportunity to watch river otters in play or fishing. We also had the chance to see short tail weasels. One short tail weasel was not afraid of us and we made no attempt to pick the critter up. We just watched it in its environment searching for tundra voles. One morning the short tail weasel decided to investigate the inside of our cabin. It had been living under our field cabin along the Karluk River, on Kodiak Island, for a few days and when we saw it at our door step it was no surprise. The small weasel decided to follow me into the cabin, but stopped just short of being in the front room. I left the door open and Pete, my co-worker on the project, and I sat at our kitchen table and watched. The weasel became playful, dancing side to side and approaching us much like domesticated ferrets do. I stomped my feet as if to chase it and it ran a few feet and then danced back at me all the while coming further into the room. This went on for about ten minutes before it tired or got bored of us and went back under the cabin.

The next morning a pair of river otters decided they would stake out our salmon weir, a kind of fence placed in rivers to manage the movement of adult salmon moving upstream and young salmon moving downstream. The otters then decided to take up residence under our cabin and all was well for the first few days. However, one early morning a battle raged under the floor of our cabin. We could hear the growling of the otters and the barking of the weasel. It must have been a real scrap, but the weasel prevailed because after five minutes the otters high tailed it for the river. The weasel stayed a few more days and then headed off to another lair.

The Lucky Whitetail

Danger lurks around every corner for deer. Predators in the woods such as coyotes, wolves, bear, bobcats, mountain lions, feral dogs and large raptors like golden eagles are willing to grab a deer for a meal. From time to time the prey escapes the predator and the deer goes on to live another day.

Predators have many different ways of catching their prey like the stealthy stalk or ambush of a mountain lion, the steady pursuit of a coyote, the organized attack of a pack of wolves or the rush of a bear. One spring we frequently saw a doe we called Lucky.

Picture 11. Doe whitetail deer with scars at base of neck and on her side. The scars are hard to see in the picture, but they are very distinct when seen through a pair of binoculars.

She carried numerous scars on her neck and sides making her easy to spot. The scars were very conspicuous when seen through binoculars or a telephoto camera. My guess is that she was attacked by a mountain lion that may have been waiting in a tree. The large predator probably dropped onto the deer's back and scrapped her sides with its claws as it ambushed the doe. The doe was lucky to have escaped and recovered from the attack.

A few years earlier, Beth and I frequently saw a young buck we called Split Ear. Split ear had a left ear that looked like someone had cut the ear in half all the way to the auditory canal. Split ear hung around our place for several years before moving on.

Don't Mess with Mama

Sow brown bears are incredibly protective of their offspring. Although brown bear attacks in north Idaho and Montana are few and far between, when they do occur it is often the accidental situation where a hunter unwittingly came between a cub and a sow. The outcome is usually one sided.

On a lazy afternoon at the Karluk Alaska cabin, I decided to watch the brown bears fish, since work was done for the day. Pete and I had names for 17 bears. The sockeye run was in full swing on the Karluk River and it was common to see two or three bears chasing salmon. On this particular afternoon I was watching Ma Brown and her cub with my binoculars. Ma Brown chased salmon while her cub played and rolled in the water. Male brown bears are well aware of male cubs and will kill them if the opportunity presents thereby preserving their own genes in the population. Ma Brown decided to move downstream and her cub raced through the shallows far out in front. I realized the cub was heading toward a spot that was occupied by an exceptionally huge bruin I named Bruno.

A month earlier, Bruno had been tranquilized by agents of the U.S. Fish and Wildlife Service as part of a radio telemetry study of bear movement. Bruno was measured before being fitted with a radio collar and was 98 inches from the tip of his tail to the tip of his nose, and 108 inches from the tip of his left toe to the tip of the right, with a 48 inch neck and weighed about 1,000 pounds.

On with the story, I knew there would be trouble and shouted to Pete to come watch. It was only a few seconds later that Bruno burst from his lair and was on target to intercept the cub. In a split second Ma Brown was on her way to an almost certain collision with Bruno. I was absolutely astounded at how fast she ran in the foot deep water. She closed the gap between her and Bruno in seconds. The cub froze at the sight of the giant Bruno coming for him. Ma Brown was ten feet in front of her cub when she stood on her hind feet and began growling. Bruno stopped within a few feet of her. Although, she was standing on her hind legs, she was only a few feet above the immense Bruno on all fours.

Bruno noted every move of the protective sow. His head bobbed up and down and then swung side to side, all the while bobbing as if he didn't know what to do. This is displacement behavior, when the situation changes drastically and the animal doesn't know how to react. Finally, Bruno gained his wits and turned and walked back to his comfortable bed in the willows while Ma Brown and her cub continued their walk downstream. Her cub, now at her side, perhaps learned a lesson. Some bear experts say, to avoid serious injury, bears know when to fight and when not to and…this was not a fight Bruno wanted to risk injury.

The Mountain Goat Versus the Grizzly

Many years ago I met an old timer who told me a story of a grizzly bear and mountain goat confrontation. He said it happened on a cliff off Bernard Peak, adjacent to Lake Pend Oreille, Idaho. He was watching a mountain goat from the lake while he was fishing. The goat was high up on a cliff when suddenly a grizzly came onto the alpine mountain side. The grizzly saw the goat and took off for it at a gallop. The two animals fought for a few minutes until they collided one too many times. They lost their balance and both fell several hundred feet to their deaths on rocks below. I guess that battle was a draw.

When I lived in Alaska, I heard a similar story of a grizzly and mountain goat fight. The goat impaled the grizzly several times with its horns, but the goat was fatally mauled by the also mortally wounded bear, both died. Mountain goats are tough, durable animals and are much larger than some people think, some goats weighing up to 300 pounds.

Terminator Ermine

Short tail weasels are also known as ermine when they're in white winter coats. If you've ever watched them, they are in perpetual motion hunting for prey or playing. One of these small creatures of only a few ounces in weight can eliminate a flock of chickens or a cage of rabbits in no time. Their sharp teeth allow them to chew through light wire on a cage and their long slinky bodies can squeeze through the slightest openings.

About 25 years ago we moved from town to the country in Idaho. The morning of our first Thanksgiving in the country I noticed a gorgeous white ermine. Of all places it was hanging on the screen outside of our dining room glass sliding door. I grabbed a camera and took a picture of it. It was apparently unafraid of me because it climbed around while on the screen and seemed in a playful mood. It eventually went on its way and we had a late afternoon family Thanksgiving dinner. With the remaining turkey in the roasting pan, I placed the pan outside on the top rail of the deck off the dining room. The next morning I found the lid pushed off and some of the turkey eaten as well as bones. The ermine popped up from behind the pan. It had a very Happy Thanksgiving dinner also.

For many years in her career, Beth cared for disabled owls, hawks and small falcons and taught about them in her wildlife education programs. They were extremely popular with the public, but their consumption of mice was incredible and expensive. Beth came up the idea of raising mice in our barn in aquariums with screen lids. There were twelve aquariums with two female mice each raising eight to ten youngsters.

Some of the aquariums with pregnant mice were used in an educational program called "Mouse House" where Beth would take the whole set up of cage, bedding, food and expectant mouse to an elementary class. Beth would present a lesson about mammals to the students and then show them how to take care of the mouse. The class would keep the little pet through the birth of the babies and their first month of life. The teacher used the program to have the students write stories about the mice, songs, "mouse math" and reading books about mammals. After the month was over, Beth would come back to the class and pick up the cage and mice, minus mice that were adopted by students. It was a very popular activity among the students.

The mouse rearing project was a success for quite a while. After all, the birds were getting fresh mice, not the frozen hormone-laced commercial kind. Then one morning Beth went to the barn and found every mouse dead in the dozen aquariums. Some small critter had chewed a small round hole through every screen lid. Nearly every mouse from the babies to the adults had their head bitten and none were eaten. It was carnage in miniature. Was it the white ermine? Beth knew that to start over in the barn would only end with the same result.

The mouse rearing project was resurrected when Beth had the idea of moving the aquariums into an old brown minivan. I removed all the seats and we set up shelves. The aquariums were in layers and the operation went on efficiently and the birds were back into fresh mice. We thought the van would be impervious to any ermine/weasel attack and we called the van, "the mouse mobile." The project was working fine and then it happened again, Beth went into the van to tend the mice and found every rodent dead again. The van was not impervious to the terminator ermine. Beth had to return to ordering frozen mice for the raptors and snakes.

Little Big Fox

Red fox on Kodiak Island are thought to be the largest anywhere in the world. One reason is the high protein salmon diet; no different from the huge size attained by coastal brown bears, once called Kodiak bears. As big as the fox are, they usually don't catch their own salmon, but steal their meals from the skilled bears that catch the fish. However, the much smaller thieving fox risks being killed by the aggressive bear. All of this occurs at a critical time for both animals. The late summer / early fall run of salmon comes just before winter when food is scarce. The bears have to hibernate with a supply of body fat while the fox needs nourishment to carry it through the harsh winter.

In 1969, I saw a few bear and red fox encounters by the Karluk River on Kodiak Island, Alaska. The fox does not fight the bear for its meal, but through quick moves steals it. If the chunk of salmon was small enough, the fox could usually sneak in when the bear wasn't looking, grab it and run with it. One such red fox was very lucky. The fox stealthily approached the bear from its blind side. The fox snuck alongside the bear and as quick as a wink, it grabbed a chunk of salmon just as the bear swiped at the small fox. The swipe just caught the back end of the fox spinning it around. The bear tried to pounce on the fox, but somehow the small thief avoided the bear's massive paws. The fox found enough space to run the opposite direction with the chunk of salmon. That is a dangerous way to make a living.

The Osprey or The Fish

Most of the museum mounts Beth had at the Wildlife Centers in Coeur d'Alene, Idaho and Manchester, Iowa were donated by sportsman, found dead in the field or on roadsides. All were accompanied by interesting and often sad stories.

Several years ago, a fisherman brought in an osprey that he found dead in a bay of Lake Coeur d'Alene. He believed it to be the same bird that he was watching as it fished the day before. The osprey was circling nearby, watching the water below and then it went into a typical power dive. Usually osprey go under the water in their dive and then resurface to come flying out with their prey. This time the bird disappeared. The fisherman waited for the osprey to surface and it never did. The next day the fisherman found a dead osprey on the shoreline of that same bay. When birds like osprey sink their talons into their prey, they may have a difficult time releasing it. The talons of birds of prey are not at all like a pair of hands that can grasp something and then release. This unfortunate bird apparently grabbed a fish far too large for it to handle. The fish felt the talons sink into its back and it swam deeper into the water pulling the osprey with it. The bird drowned and its talons released in death and the body floated onto the shore. Some fisherman have told us that they have caught large fish that show scars on their back – scars that have the same arrangement of a raptors talons.

Without Warning

By now you should be convinced animals in the wild have a daily survival challenge and must ensure the survival of their offspring. While I was working for ADFG watching bears chase and catch salmon was a frequent pastime. At the same time we were watching bears, we'd see an occasional merlin fly up or down the river. They'd hug the river's contour and sweep through at high speeds, any unsuspecting shore bird was usually a goner. The shore birds never had an opportunity to flee, the merlins were so quick they'd hit the shore bird without warning. The merlin usually fed on the victim in place or carried it to a nearby bush (there were no trees).

I have only seen one or two rare peregrine falcons. The most memorable peregrine falcon story occurred. A friend told me he was watching a crow flying by the Monarch cliffs near Lake Pend Oreille. Then a peregrine falcon came into view above the crow. The peregrine dropped from above in a stoop attack (peregrine falcons are thought to hit speeds of 180 miles per hour in stoop attacks). The peregrine had extended his feet and talons at the last second and the impact literally exploded the crow in air. In midair the peregrine caught the dead free falling crow, carried it to tree on shore and ate it.

A HELPING HAND

Bully

We lived in rural northeast Iowa for almost 14 years where Beth worked as the County Conservation Education Coordinator and managed a beautiful nature center. One pleasant afternoon Beth was going to town to take a music lesson. There on the side of the road was a dead snake. She drove her vehicle to the side of the road and walked to the dead bull snake (known as gopher snake in the west). Beth envisioned an exhibit of a snake skeleton for the nature center.

The snake had been hit on the side of its head by the wheel of a passing vehicle, but was otherwise undamaged. Beth did not particularly like snakes, but thought the educational benefit of the skeleton would be of value. However, Beth didn't have a box to transport the snake in so she removed her guitar from the case and scooped the bull snake into it and latched it shut. After her music lesson Beth came home and set the guitar case down, with the dead snake in it, in the garage intending to deal with it the next day.

The next evening Beth went into the garage and opened the lid on the case. The "dead" bull snake lifted its head and stared at Beth. An astonished Beth quickly shut the lid. That was the last thing she expected. Now what to do? The bull snake was still alive and Beth felt responsible for its care. The bull snake had a broken jaw and if it were released it would die, so hand feeding it would be necessary. The snake was force fed by holding its mouth open and slipping food into its gullet. Once the food was pushed into its throat, the swallow reflex took over and food went into its stomach. The snake was docile and Beth warmed up to the serpent more and more as she cared for it.

The snake was named Bully and became one of the most popular live animals at the nature center. With Beth's care the snake lived for many years and totally revered Beth's feeling about snakes. She eventually added many more snakes to the center including a timber rattle snake, a 6-foot black rat snake, two fox snakes, a blue racer, two species of garter snakes, a northern water snake, and a hog-nosed snake. Bully not only changed Beth's perception of snakes, but during her years at the nature center thousands of visitors handled and admired this extraordinary creature God had provided to our good earth.

Some Snakes Lay Eggs

When Beth was the manager of the Wildlife Center in Iowa, she had a display of live native snakes. One of the cages held two fox snakes. The two snakes had been together for several years in the large cage that had green indoor / outdoor carpeting, a water bowl and a small hollow log for the snakes to crawl into. One summer day, Beth noticed that the carpeting that lined the cage and usually laid flat against the bottom was bunched up in the center of the cage. It was time to clean the cage, so Beth removed the two 2 ft. snakes and placed them into another container. When Beth picked up the rumpled carpet, she was amazed. The two fox snakes had mated and the female had laid eggs under the carpet.

Beth found a bucket and filled it with sand. She placed the eggs in the sand and put a heating lamp on it during the day hours to simulate the summer sun. If the eggs stayed in the cage with the fox snakes, they probably would not hatch, since the temperature of the cage was not ideal. Beth rotated the eggs occasionally and kept the temperature and light on the eggs as close to natural conditions as possible. She placed a screened lid on the bucket so she would not lose any hatchlings if they arrived early. Finally, the time frame in which the snakes might hatch arrived. With a video camera in hand every day, Beth saw some movement among the eggs. Little tears in the rubbery eggs started to appear and then tiny snake heads pushed through the openings. Finally, some baby fox snakes wriggled out of their shells. Not all of the eggs hatched, but most of them did produce young. After they hatched, Beth knew they would need to be set free to find the food that they needed to survive. She took the reptiles to a remote wooded area in the park that was close to water, brush, and trees and watched them wiggle away.

Some Snakes Have Live Births

In Idaho, Beth managed a Wildlife Center for 22 years and the snakes there were one of the more popular attractions. The snakes that lived there were rubber boas. Rubber boas are native to the northwest United States and are one of only two species of boas in North America. The other species is the rosy boa that is found along the Pacific coastal regions. The rubber boa is a brownish to olive colored snake with a cream colored belly and may grow to two feet in length.

The rubber boa became one of Beth's favorite reptiles when a friend brought in a large boa that had been found in the friend's yard sunning itself on a stone wall. Beth made a new home for the snake with a large aquarium outfitted with moss, stones, water bowl and small log. The snake ate insects and pinkies (new born mice) and it seemed to get bigger as the days passed. When the boa had been in the Wildlife Center for about a month, Beth noticed that there were four pinkish earthworms in the cage with the snake. She thought that someone had visited the Center and placed the worms in with the boa. Upon closer inspection, Beth saw that they were tiny snakes about four inches long and thick as a pencil. The original boa was still in the cage, but now she was thinner. The rubber boa had given live birth to four young.

What would they eat? Would the mother eat the babies? Beth put the young in another aquarium and bought small crickets, mealworms and other insects for the small boas. The baby boas started to grow and soon were fed pinkie mice. Beth knew that she could not care for five snakes at this time, so she decided to release the large boa and three of the youngsters back to the wild. The one baby boa that Beth kept was named Ruby and it lived at the Center and grew to a mature size. Ruby was a hit with children and adults alike during the nature classes and fair events held at the Wildlife Center. Over the years, other boas shared the same cage with Ruby and one year Ruby had four baby boas of its own which Beth raised. The boas became ambassadors for wildlife and especially for misunderstood animals such as snakes and other reptiles.

George

The most memorable and remarkable animal that we took care of was George, a great horned owl. George came into our lives in April 2013 when a neighbor reported to us that she had seen a small owl in a nearby field. She believed the owlet was blown out of a nest during a recent storm.

Our neighbor found the wet owlet not too far from where it had been seen a day earlier and put in a box with a dry towel. Beth dried it off even more and thought it was on the brink of death when he was found (taking wildlife from the wild is illegal unless you are a licensed rehabber). Beth placed the weeks old owlet in a small dog carrier with a soft towel and a plush toy which the bird snuggled close to. The owlet took immediately to being fed newborn mice and water. The owlet was soon named George by one of Beth's volunteers. George became a classroom favorite and grew rapidly.

George lived in a large cage and his environment, as well as the living conditions of the other disabled raptors, was carefully controlled with water-misters and fans when necessary. George had an absolutely ravenous appetite, soon switching to whole adult mice and feeding and drinking on his own. George would clack his beak and make an unusual sound we called his begging call when he wanted attention or to be fed. All of the captive birds were fed vitamin supplements as well as mice. When George's flight feathers developed, Beth exercised the owl to develop his flying muscles.

In mid-August about five months after Beth rescued him, it was obvious George was ready to be acclimated to the wild and released. Beth took George in a large pet carrier to a deer stand in the woods near our home. For two days he was fed and watered daily in his cage as he adjusted to the new surroundings. Then Beth opened the cage door and George stepped out, looked around and flew out into the trees. Even though Beth did not expect to see the owl again, she still put some mice and water out for him at the platform. Checking the platform the next day, Beth saw that George's mice were untouched. We figured we did our job and now it was up to him to survive on his own.

Two days after George flew away, Beth was out in the horse corral talking to the horse and llama when she heard a familiar call – a begging call. George had heard Beth's voice and was back for food. Beth saw the owl flying in from the wooded area to a tree close to the corral. She said his name and he called back. Beth brought some mice from the animal freezer, warmed them and set them on a flat rock at the edge of the corral. She watched from a distance as the great horned owl swooped down and picked up the mice. Every evening for the next four months, George returned and called to get our attention. He moved his location from the trees at the edge of the woods to the posts of the corral to the roof of our house and then finally to the railing of our kitchen deck.

One night when we did not hear or see him before we went to bed, the owl appeared on the railing of the deck outside our bedroom. He was looking through the glass door and then started his begging call. When Beth got up to get some mice, George flew around the other side of the house where Beth fed him at the railing of the kitchen deck. Another time, Beth was a little late in getting his mice ready and George landed on the window AC just on the other side of the kitchen window where Beth was washing dishes and stared at her. Beth would call George's name in the evening and the large owl would fly to the railing and sit and chatter with her as she held out the mice. If there were any other people around, George would not come by until they were gone. Some times when we had family or friends over, Beth would turn off the house lights and put on the outside porch light when she placed mice on the railing and George would make a quick stop on the railing, grab the mice and then fly away.

Around January, there was a snowfall and we did not see George for a few weeks. We figured he was either a victim of the harsh elements or had enough of us. To our surprise George was back to us in mid-January for several weeks and then he would be gone for a week or two. We thought that it easier to learn to hunt while the snow on the ground made prey more visible. Once spring arrived, George was visiting us every night again until the next years snowfall.

That summer George developed a peculiar habit of stealing towels we left outside to dry. He'd hang them in trees and from time to time move them from one tree to another. He had as many as three towels in our trees at one time. In fact there is still a towel in one of our trees left behind by George (April 2018). What this behavior meant I have no idea, but perhaps he was just being playful. It was also curious that George continued with his baby begging call for a long time. Then in summer of 2015 he started to hoot at us.

George spent the rest of 2015 and most of 2016 around our home and often went missing only to return. Each time that he disappeared, it was for longer periods, up to two months at a time. But, by December 2016 George took off for good. Perhaps he found a mate. Some people don't believe a raptor raised in captivity and released to the wild can survive, but it can be done.

From time to time I hear great horned owls calling in the evening. Perhaps to call a mate, give their location or warn others to stay clear of their territory. I always like to think one of the callers is George and that he and a mate raised a brood of great horned owlets.

Picture 12. George as an adult great horned owl after his release.

Beware of Beaks

After serving two years in the Army and two and a half years in graduate school, I was hired by the Iowa Conservation Commission as a fish management trainee. My assignment was with the Chariton Research Station. One of the first things I noticed as I entered my new office building was a mounted great blue heron. It was a nuisance because it was mounted with its beak facing straight out. If a person cut a corner too sharply, their pant leg would catch on the bird and spin it around.

One day curiosity got the better of me and I asked about the history of the bird. As the story goes the bird was seriously injured when hit by a car. A passerby picked the bird up and put it in a box and delivered it to a local veterinarian. The vet was told what was in the box and that the bird was near death. He opened the box and took hold of the bird to move it to see the extent of its injuries. The frightened bird promptly poked the vet in the right eye - permanently blinding him. The vet later said he held no grudge with the bird and warned people to use extreme caution when handling any wildlife.

A year after I heard the story of the unfortunate veterinarian, I was asked to go get an injured great blue heron. I brought a large fish net and made sure my face never got close to the bird. I brought it to a vet in a large box and cautioned him. The vet did not need a warning because he was all too familiar with the story on the mounted bird. Then in Idaho I was asked to untangle fishing line from the feet and body of a great blue heron that was hobbled on the shores of Fernan Lake. Beth assisted me. The bird was indeed wrapped up with fishing line and once again we were cautious. We safely untangled the bird from a mess of fishing line and it flew off.

A Lucky Buck

Friends Bill and Shirley had just moved to north Idaho when two neighbors asked them to help free a deer from certain death. The buck had tangled its antlers in fencing and had struggled for hours to get free. The trapped buck was reported to IDFG, but when Bill and Shirley learned it would be hours before someone could respond they decided to take things into their own hands.

Each of the four rescuers had an assignment; two would hold the buck down, one would hold a blanket over the buck's eyes and when the exhausted buck was under control, another would cut the fencing. After a few minutes, the buck was freed and the liberators stepped back to give the animal plenty of room. However, instead of bounding off as expected the fatigued deer laid down. It was a long time before the buck finally regained enough strength and slowly walked to the nearby woods.

Releasing animals is a noble thing when the authorities are unable to do it, but extreme caution and good planning as in the above story should be used. Stressed animals can be very dangerous and many well intentioned people have been seriously injured by frightened animals.

Picture 13. Whitetail buck stuck in a fence and freed by Bill and Shirlee and two neighbors.

Baby the Barred Owl

Laws are in place to prevent unlicensed and inexperienced people from keeping young or disabled wildlife and this next story is a good example. A family brought two half-grown barred owlets in to the Wildlife Center in Idaho with a story that they had just found them. The owlets were in a box and the people left in a hurry without giving their names. Beth opened the box, inside were two young, but very sick barred owlets. The owlets were obviously malnourished, their beaks were crossed instead of the normal alignment and the toes on their feet were tightly curled in. The birds could not use their feet to perch. One of the owlets was in worse condition than the other. It laid in the box.

From the condition of the two birds, it appeared that they had been deprived of essential vitamins and minerals for quite a long time. If the two birds had just been found, then the parent owls would have been feeding the owlets and they would not have had a severe calcium deficiency. The most obvious answer to the birds condition was that they were kept by people who did not have a clue. The only thing that these people probably knew about owls was that they ate meat. I imagine that the ill-intentioned people fed the owlets ground beef, bits of raw chicken, or other types of meat. The baby birds most likely gobbled up the food, but weeks without the calcium and other minerals that the bones in wild prey food provide, the owlets started to show the signs of malnourishment. That was most likely the point in which the captors of the owls got scared and needed to turn them in to someone – with a bogus story too.

The owlets were fed supplements and given water immediately. Unfortunately, one of the siblings died during the night leaving one deformed barred owlet that Beth named Baby. We didn't think Baby would survive and if it did live we didn't think its feet would recover, straighten or ever be able to grasp a perch or even prey. However, to our delight Baby proved us wrong. Its feet gradually uncurled, so he could grasp a perch, stand on his own and hold food. Its beak also straightened out and became stronger. Baby grew rapidly and started to test his wings. We let him fly around in our garage and swoop down from the rafters to pick up dead mice from the floor. Eventually Baby was ready to turn loose.

The young owl was fledged gradually by placing it in a large pet carrier set on a tree stand in our woods. After a couple of days, the bird was free to leave. A large pan of water and food (mice) were also placed on the tree stand. Baby roosted in trees near the stand for several days before it no longer used the pan or ate the mice. Over the next two weeks we would see Baby from time to time in trees because it would make a hissing call notifying us of its presence. Occasionally, the owl would come to the tree stand to pick up some mice, until finally the mice were no longer needed. Eventually our visual contact with Baby ended and we believed he was on his own.

Several weeks went by when our son and his companions camped on our property. The boys decided to take an afternoon hike downhill to a Lake Coeur d'Alene boat launch. When evening came the boys decided to return uphill to their campsite. They noticed on the way up that a very bold barred owl was following them. It flew from tree to tree as they made their way up the road to the campsite. Baby roosted in a nearby tree that evening, but was gone the next morning.

The following weekend we gave the okay to a seasonal worker for one of the government agencies to camp one evening in our woods. We never mentioned to this worker anything about the remarkable owl that we had released nearly two months earlier. The next day when the young man came into work, he excitedly told us that a barred owl had flown around his camp site, perched on a tree branch for almost an hour and then landed on the roof of his vehicle. It turned out that the camper was also a birder and he had never seen a barred owl before and needed to add one to his life list. No wonder he was so thrilled.

We were sure that the owl was likely Baby in both circumstances.

She Sleeps with the Fishes

He sleeps with the fishes is a Sicilian metaphor for someone that went missing and was executed by the Mob. My first published short novel is called They Sleep with the Fishes. It's based off true stories of my family's involvement with the Mob during the Great Depression. In the book I tell how three goons tried to extort my grandfather and how a Mob boss came to his aide by sending them to the bottom of Lake Michigan to sleep with the fishes. Many of my friends read the book including my friend Jim.

Jim lives in rural north Idaho and has a cat that hunts ground squirrels. One morning Jim's cat brought a dead ground squirrel home and dropped it on his back patio. Before the dead rodent could be removed his very young granddaughter saw it and asked Jim what it was doing there. Jim simply explained it was sleeping with the fishes. Later that day the little girl's mother took a nap and was sleeping in bed. When the child was asked by her grandmother where the mother was, she said, "Mommy is sleeping with the fishes."

The Things That Kids Say

Throughout the nearly forty years of Beth's career as a Conservation Educator, she has been privileged to interact and learn from people aged 1 to 91. Usually the questions and answers from the audiences are the same questions and answers that have been asked over the years. However, once in a while there is the unexpected. Below are just a few of the many "surprise" comments that the young and "young at heart" have come up with.

While narrating during eagle cruises, Beth typically keeps her audience involved by asking questions. One beautiful December afternoon she was talking about the life history of eagles to 5th graders and asked if anyone knew why eagles came to the Wolf Lodge Bay / Beauty Bay area of Lake Coeur d'Alene. One young man raised his hand and was called on. He proudly said, "The eagles were eating salmon."

"That is correct," Beth said. The next question was, "What kind of salmon do the eagles eat at this time of year."

"Smoked salmon," he responded.

In the mid 1990's our town used to have a home improvement store called Eagle Hardware. The store had a poster to advertise its products and the poster featured a large eagle picture. I cut the store name from the poster and used the eagle print with my presentations about the eagle. One day, I visited a nursing home to talk about eagles. I brought several large mounted eagles, bald and golden, to show the residents. The audience came in and sat down and just before it was time to start, one last elderly gentleman came into the room and looked at the display of birds. "What is this?" he demanded. I told him we were going to talk about the National Symbol of the United States. "I thought this was a program about tools," he answered angrily before he turned and shuffled out of the room.

Occasionally Vaughn and our friend Rich taught a class about fish to second graders. The two instructors talked about some species of native fish, some fishing techniques and some food items of fish. To engage the students in thinking about fish, Vaughn or Rich would ask if the students liked to fish? Most kids responded yes to that question. Then one of the men asked what do you like to fish for? A third grade boy answered with all sincerity,

"Fish sticks!" The following session with a different group of students, the same question was asked and a boy answered—fish sticks. Rich tried to catch him off guard and asked, "Where do you like to fish for fish sticks?" The boy answered, "In my mom's freezer."

At another program about "Mammals," Beth described the characteristics of mammal skulls and the different teeth in the skull. Canine teeth (the sharp teeth in the corners of an animal's mouth) helped the mammals tear meat and molars (the flat block-like teeth in the back of the mouth) are mostly for chewing plant material as plants may be harder to chew than meat (think tree bark or plant stems). Beth held up a picture of a muskrat and asked the class if that mammal had canine teeth or molars or both. There were varied answers until Beth told the class that muskrats eat mostly vegetation such as pond plants, water lilies, plant roots and cattails and are considered herbivores. Most of the class then decided that muskrats must have several molars, but no canine teeth. One young student waved his hand insistently and then declared that muskrats must have canine teeth. "Why do you think so?" Beth asked. The student replied, "Because it eats cat's tails."

Beth also taught students in first through third grade about animal habitats in the forests, especially snags (dead or dying trees) that can be used for homes, feeding areas, nesting or other purposes by more than 460 animals. She described how wood ducks used holes (cavities) in dead trees to nest and lay their clutch of eggs. Sometimes the cavities are high in the trunk of the tree, even 60 plus feet. One student listened intently and then asked. "How do the baby wood ducks get out of the tree if the hole is so high from the ground?" I described how the ducklings climb to the cavity edge and then jump out and since they are quite fluffy, they float to the ground and could even bounce when they land. The same student pondered that for a moment and said, "I don't know how they could survive that jump, they would die." I assured the young boy that the ducklings are able to survive and follow their mother duck to the nearest water. The student just shook his head in disbelief.

Later in the discussion about snags, I asked the class how they would be able to distinguish a snag from any other tree. The students raised their hands and told their ideas. "It is a dead or dying tree." "There are cavities in the snag." "The bark may be gone from the snag." "The branches may be mostly missing." "There are bugs around the trunk or burrows near the roots." The student, who had his doubts about the fate of the ducklings, waved his hand in the air. He answered, "There is a pile of dead baby wood ducks on the ground in front of it."

The old saying that, "If you do something that you love for a *living*, you never *work* a day in your life," is certainly true. Wildlife *work* was many things, but it was never dull.

The Most Outrageous Tale of All

We finished this book with an outrageous story. One of my best high school buddies, Gene, had an awesome mom. She made Gene sandwiches for snacks before baseball practices. On one particular day, Gene didn't want a snack that day. A teammate mentioned how hungry he was so Gene offered him the sandwich. His teammate accepted it, took a bite and spit it out all over the locker room floor. He asked Gene who made the sandwich. Gene said his mother. Gene's teammate said, "Your mother, what kind of a mother do you have? It's full of coffee grounds." One of the more curious points in Gene's mother-son relationship was that they were continuously playing jokes on each other. Oh by the way, that day was April Fool's Day.

One day, I became an unsuspecting part of a joke Gene pulled on his mom. Gene was a novice outdoorsman and whenever I invited him on one of my adventures he readily accepted. On a Friday afternoon Gene and I traveled to my family's cabin in central Wisconsin. For the following day, I planned a morning of bow fishing for carp with an afternoon of largemouth bass fishing. So Saturday, we shared my "Bear" fifty-nine pound recurve bow and bow-fished for carp. Carp were spawning in my favorite bay, we bow-fished for them all morning and caught a few. It was Gene's turn with the bow and as he drew on several carp spawning on the surface, he wasn't quick enough and they ducked out of sight. Simultaneously three carp rolled to his left and I shouted, "Gene shoot left." He turned quickly and released prematurely and let out a yell. The released bowstring ripped across his left forearm leaving an ugly red welt. That was enough bow fishing for him due to the worst bow string bruise I had ever seen. We switched to largemouth bass fishing, something he had never done. I set him up with a nice rod and reel and my favorite top water lure, a Creek Chub Injured Minnow armed with three large treble hooks. I brought our boat into some lily pads and pointed out good spots to cast the lure. A few minutes later I heard a big bass grab Gene's lure. He immediately asked me what to do. I excitedly shouted, "Set the hook." Gene jerked the fishing rod excessively hard and the empty lure came out of the water. The lure was sailing straight toward Gene's head, quickly he swung his head to avoid being hit in the face. The lure hit him on the left shoulder and all three treble hooks set into his arm.

Again he let out a yell that could have been heard down to Wisconsin Dells. I saw the hooks impaled in his arm and told him to hold still. Although the hooks were deep, none sank in beyond the barb and I was able to remove them.

Gene then asked, "Where are my glasses?" They had flown off his head when he turned to avoid having the lure sink into his face. His glasses weren't in the boat so they had to be in the water. The water was only four feet deep so Gene stripped down to his undies and into the water he went to feel for his glasses with his feet. He had no success. He searched again the next morning and couldn't find the glasses. We decided to call it a weekend and drove south to Racine where we lived.

I dropped Gene at his home and he invited me over after supper to shoot pool with him in his recreation room. I took him up on the offer. Later that evening, when I returned to his house, I was greeted by Gene's mother. She said, "Vaughn, I want to thank you for saving Gene's life. He told me what you did. Diving into the water with a knife in your mouth and then chopping the giant sea lamprey off his arm was a brave thing to do." A sea lamprey is an eel-like primitive fish. I was not expecting Gene to make up a story and make me the hero. I said, "I'm sure Gene would have done the same for me. We take care of each other." She thanked me again. I went down stairs to Gene's recreation room and asked what he told his mom. He said he told her a huge bass took his lure and when he set the hook too hard the lure flew out of the water at his face. So he swung his head and the lure hit his shoulder, but his glasses sailed into the water.

Gene continued the story that he told his mother, "Vaughn removed the hooks from my shoulder and then I went into the water to find my glasses. While I was underwater searching for my glasses, a giant sea lamprey latched onto my arm. I struggled to get to the surface to breath, but the huge creature was pulling me deeper. That's when Vaughn immediately took action, put a Bowie knife between his teeth and dived head first into the water. Vaughn found me submerged, took the knife from his mouth and proceeded to free me from the bloodthirsty lamprey by slicing it off my arm." Gene's mother again thanked me profusely as I left that evening.

Yes indeed, that was one of the most heroic things I had ever done.

Epilogue

Our parting message is to respect wildlife from a distance and respect their need to have a place to live. Also, enjoy the outdoors and remember the only way to experience your own wildlife tales is to get outdoors.

About the Authors

Vaughn L. and Elizabeth (Beth) Paragamian were married in June of 1972. They met in a disco club in January of 1971 and had common ground immediately after they started telling each other animal stories. Vaughn was born in Kenosha, Wisconsin where he and his family lived with his Italian grandparents for several years. His family moved to Racine where he spent much time with his Armenian paternal grandmother. Vaughn spent most of his free time on or near the Root River while growing up. He had an inquisitive nose for science and biology and enjoys sports. He has a BS from Iowa State University and an MS from the University of Wisconsin, Stevens Point. Vaughn worked for Alaska, Wisconsin, Iowa and Idaho fish and game departments. He is a veteran, having served in the Army from 1969 -1971. He spent 42 years as a fisheries research scientist and enjoyed scientific writing. Vaughn retired from the Idaho Department of Fish and Game (IDFG) in 2011. He has the nickname 'The Codfather' and has authored several other books; *They Sleep with the Fishes, Trust Only Family* and *Eye of the Cobra*.

Beth was born in Baltimore, Maryland. She enjoyed playing sports in school and was an excellent student. She had many jobs while growing up including babysitting and as a camp counselor. She put herself through college working as a waitress on weekends and has a BA from Towson State University majoring in Biology, Chemistry and Education. She taught school for a short time in Wisconsin and Iowa before taking a job as a Wildlife Educator in Iowa and then in Idaho with Idaho Department of Fish and Game (IDFG), US Forest Service and US Bureau of Land Management (BLM) for a combined total of 39 years. She received many awards for her educational skills from federal agencies, wildlife groups and civic groups including 1999 Woman of the Year in Education from three area universities, 2009 BLM's National Educator of the Year and 2018 Wildlife Educator of the Year from Kootenai Environmental Alliance. Beth retired from the IDFG in 2018, but still continues to answer calls from schools, community groups, camps and agencies for wildlife presentations. Beth and Vaughn have three married children, Laura, Jon and Karin and five grandchildren. The authors live near Coeur d'Alene, Idaho with their dogs Daisy and Enrico.